Maths Spotlight

Pupil Book

3

Heinemann

Series editor	Peter Clarke
Consultant	Len Frobisher
Writing team	Janine Blinko
	Paula Coombes
	Hilary Koll
	Steve Mills
	Jeanette Mumford

Heinemann Educational Publishers
Halley Court, Jordan Hill, Oxford, OX2 8EJ
a division of Harcourt Education Ltd
www.heinemann.co.uk

Heinemann is a registered trademark of Harcourt Education Ltd

First published 2002

06 05 04 03 02
10, 9, 8, 7, 6, 5, 4, 3, 2, 1

ISBN 0 435 20610 9

Illustrated by Derek Matthews
Cover illustration by Dave Cockburn
Cover design by Paul Goodman
Designed by Paul Davies and Associates
Printed in Spain by Edelvives

Contents

Let's practise

1 How many?

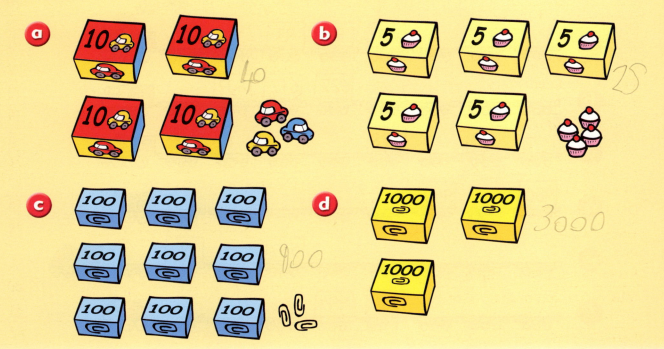

a 40

b 25

c 900

d 3000

Let's investigate

2 Work with a partner.

- Cut the paper into strips.

- Stick strips end to end until you have a strip that reaches across your table.

- Draw a red line at the end of every 5 squares, and a black line at the end of every 10 squares.

- Find out how many squares are in your strip by counting in 5s.

- Check your answer by counting in 10s.

- Together decide how long you think a strip with 1000 squares would be.

- Make a strip of 1000 squares by adding more squares to your strip.

> **You need**
>
> centimetre squared paper, scissors, sticky tape

Let's practise

1 Copy and complete the sequences.

a | 73 | 83 | 93

b | 627 | 617 | 607

c | 378 | | 578

d | 960 | | 940

e | 537 | | 737

f | 984 | 994

Let's investigate

2 Work with a partner.

Take turns to:

- Roll all 3 dice and use the numbers to make a 3-digit start number.

- Count on in 100s from your number until you pass 1000.

- Your partner checks with the calculator:

| + | 1 | 0 | 0 | = | = | = |

- Both record your numbers.

- Check to see if you each got the same numbers.

Change the rules:

- Count back in 100s.

- Stop after 8 numbers or when you pass 0.

Let's practise

1 Janet and Sanjay tried to sort some numbers.

Odd	Even	Neither odd nor even
57	44	0
26	81	
3	8	
7	58	

Make a table like this and sort the numbers correctly.
Add some more numbers to your table.

Let's investigate

2 Take these 3 digit cards: **5** **6** **7**

> **You need**
> digit cards for numbers 0 to 9

Odd	Even

- Use them to make 6 different 3-digit numbers.
- Write the numbers in a table.

a How many odd numbers do you have?

b How many even numbers?

c Explain why there is a different number of each.

3 Choose another 3 digit cards so that you can make more even numbers than odd numbers.

4 Is it possible to choose 3 digit cards so that the number of even numbers and the number of odd numbers is the same? Explain why.

Let's practise

1 Write the missing numbers for each scale.

a
600 ml

200 ml
100 ml

b
600 ml

100 ml

c
350 ml
300 ml

100 ml

d
1000 ml

400 ml
200 ml

Let's investigate

2 ● Draw a number line.

● Write a 3-digit multiple of 100 at one end and the next multiple of 100 at the other end.

400 　　　　　　　　　　　　　 500

● Write the number half way between the 2 numbers.

400 　　　　　　450　　　　　　500

● Draw as many different number lines like this as you can.

❓ What if you had a multiple of 50 at one end and the next multiple of 50 at the other?

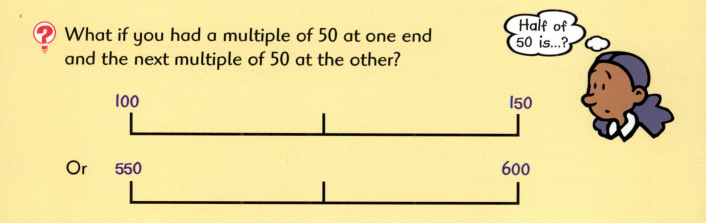

Half of 50 is...?

100 　　　　　　　　　　　　　 150

Or 　 550 　　　　　　　　　　　　 600

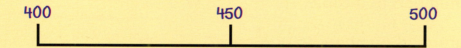

Let's practise

1

-150   -125   -100   -75   -50   -25   0   25   50   75

Write the numbers that are 25 more and 25 less than each of these.

a 100   **b** –75   **c** 300   **d** –225

e 25   **f** 125   **g** –25   **h** 575

i –100   **j** –200   **k** 525   **l** 0

2 ● Draw a grid with 10 rows.

● Make it big enough for counters to fit. You will use it for the game.

● Fill in the missing numbers.

● Stop when you reach 1000.

25	50	75	100
125	150	175	200
225	250		

			1000

Let's play   A game for 2

● Each cover 3 numbers on your own grid with counters.

● Take turns to say which numbers your partner has covered.

● On your grid colour the numbers you said correctly.

● The winner is the first to colour 21 numbers.

You need

3 counters, your completed grid from question 2, a coloured pencil

175

Let's practise

1 Copy and complete these sequences.

(a) ▢   213   223   233   243   253   ▢

(b) ▢   999   899   799   699   599   ▢

(c) ▢   13   10   7   4   1   ▢

(d) ▢   1025   1030   1035   1040   1045   ▢

(e) ▢   9   7   5   3   1   ▢

(f) ▢   326   330   334   338   342   ▢

Let's investigate

2

(a) Choose one of the numbers on the cars.
Write a sequence that has your number as its middle number.

(b) Choose any 2 of the numbers.
Write a sequence that has your numbers as the end numbers.

(c) Choose any 3 of the numbers.
Write a sequence that has your numbers in it.

?   What if the numbers on the cars were all negative?

Let's practise

1 Write the numbers that are multiples of 5.

Boats with numbers: 11, 253, 58, 215, 845, 91, 500, 550, 235, 130, 200, 531, 375, 1000

Let's investigate

2 Choose any whole number from 1 to 10.

- Use it in the middle of a sequence, counting on or back in 5s.

−18 −13 −8 −3 2 **7** 12 17 22 27 32

> I chose 7. My sequence is made by counting in 5s.

- Write 5 numbers on either side of your middle number.

- Write about patterns in the units digits.

- Write about any other patterns you notice.

Choose a different start number.

 What if the sequence was made by counting in 10s?

Let's practise

1 Find a number on the line to match each statement.

a A multiple of 2 and of 3, greater than 6.

b A multiple of 2 but not a multiple of 3.

c A multiple of 4 and of 5.

d A multiple of 5 but not a multiple of 10.

e A multiple of 4 and of 3, greater than 12.

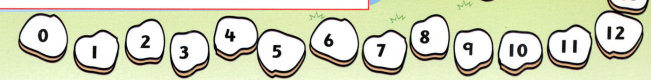

Let's play   A game for 2

- Turn over 4 cards each.
- Put counters on your cards following these rules:
  2 counters if the number is a multiple of 2.
  3 counters if the number is a multiple of 3.
  4 counters if the number is a multiple of 4.
  5 counters if the number is a multiple of 5.
  10 counters if the number is a multiple of 10.
- The winner is the player with more counters.
- Play 5 times.

Who is the overall winner?

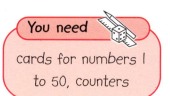

You need

cards for numbers 1 to 50, counters

Let's practise

1 Copy and write these numbers in figures.

a Two thousand nine hundred and twenty-two

b Four thousand five hundred and sixty-seven

c Six thousand one hundred and nineteen

d Five thousand six hundred and twenty

e Three thousand one hundred and four

f One thousand and twenty-seven

g Eleven thousand and forty-five

h Twenty-six thousand and six

2 Copy and write these numbers in words.

a 2781 **b** 4827 **c** 5727 **d** 7881

e 7701 **f** 2801 **g** 5787 **h** 2780

Let's solve problems

3 Find a 3- or 4-letter word for each number in question 2.

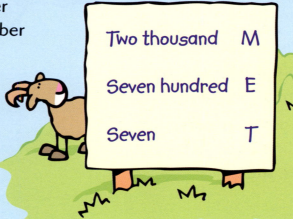

Two thousand M

Seven hundred E

Seven T

4 Write some different words using the letters.

Which number does each word stand for?

Seven thousand	B
Five thousand	W
Four thousand	L
Two thousand	M
Eight hundred	A
Seven hundred	E
Eighty	N
Twenty	S
Seven	T
One	D

Let's practise

1 Write what each red digit stands for.   4719 ⟶ 700

- **a** 4371
- **b** 5206
- **c** 7890
- **d** 3952
- **e** 6002
- **f** 4013
- **g** 8200
- **h** 5372

2 Copy and partition each number.   1709 ⟶ 1000 + 700 + 9

- **a** 4613
- **b** 7802
- **c** 3247
- **d** 1059
- **e** 9050
- **f** 6084
- **g** 2708
- **h** 5926

3 Write all the numbers between **5000** and **5100** that have a digit 4.

Let's investigate

4 The digits 5, 3, 7 and 2 have fallen off this car.

- **a** Write 10 numbers that use all 4 digits.
- **b** What is the largest possible number?
- **c** What is the smallest?
- **d** What numbers between 2735 and 3275 could it be? Write each one in words.
- **e** Write all the numbers with a thousands digit of 5. How many are there?

? What if the digits 8, 5, 1 and 1 had fallen off the car?

Let's practise

1 Copy and complete by writing < or > instead of ⬤.

   a 59 ⬤ 95

   b 81 ⬤ 18

   c 415 ⬤ 451

   d 297 ⬤ 279

   e 1000 ⬤ 999

   f 4136 ⬤ 4316

Remember the crocodile opens its jaws towards the larger number.

2 Copy and complete.

   a 23 < ▢

   b 49 > ▢

   c 57 < ▢

9 14

3 Copy and complete by writing <, > or = instead of ⬤.

   a 30 + 70 ⬤ 80 + 20

   b 156 + 19 ⬤ 211 − 89

   c 60 x 4 ⬤ 600 ÷ 5

   d 350 − 200 ⬤ 50 x 3

4 Copy and complete.

   a 39 < ▢ < 42

   b 510 < ▢ < 520

   c ▢ < 17 < ▲

   d ▢ < 1000 < ▲

Let's investigate

5 Find as many different solutions as you can for the missing numbers.

   a 3 + ▢ < 2 x ▲

   b 50 ÷ ▢ < 30 − ▲

What if the order of the operations in question 5 was changed?

Let's practise

1 Estimate how far each rider will have cycled when they pass the arrow.

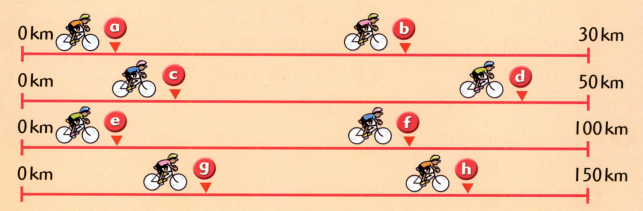

2 Estimate how many sweets are in each jar.
The number on the lid shows how many were in each full jar.

Let's play   A game for 2

- Choose something to estimate with a friend, like the number of tiles on the floor, cubes in a bag or pages in a book.
- Take turns to estimate.
- Write down your estimate.
- Now count the things.
- Whoever is closer scores 1 point.
- The winner is the first to score 5 points.

Let's practise

1 Round to the nearest 10 miles.

 **a** 79 miles **b** 156 miles **c** 482 miles

d 304 miles **e** 609 miles **f** 995 miles

2 Round the milometers to the nearest 100 miles.

a
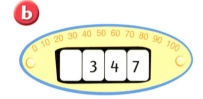
0 10 20 30 40 50 60 70 80 90 100
4 7 0

b
0 10 20 30 40 50 60 70 80 90 100
3 4 7

c
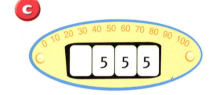
0 10 20 30 40 50 60 70 80 90 100
5 5 5

d

0 10 20 30 40 50 60 70 80 90 100
8 5 1

e
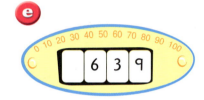
0 10 20 30 40 50 60 70 80 90 100
6 3 9

f
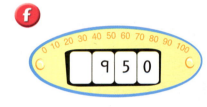
0 10 20 30 40 50 60 70 80 90 100
9 5 0

Let's investigate

3 **a** Find all the whole numbers that become 310 when rounded to the nearest 10.

b How many such numbers are there?

c Investigate for other decade numbers.

Let's practise

1 Write the temperature shown on each thermometer in °C.

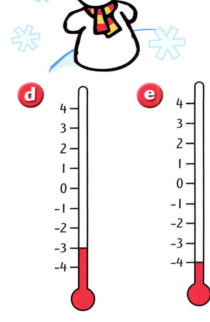

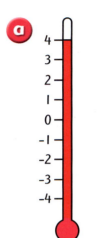

a

| 4 |
| 3 |
| 2 |
| 1 |
| 0 |
| –1 |
| –2 |
| –3 |
| –4 |

b

| 4 |
| 3 |
| 2 |
| 1 |
| 0 |
| –1 |
| –2 |
| –3 |
| –4 |

c

| 4 |
| 3 |
| 2 |
| 1 |
| 0 |
| –1 |
| –2 |
| –3 |
| –4 |

d

| 4 |
| 3 |
| 2 |
| 1 |
| 0 |
| –1 |
| –2 |
| –3 |
| –4 |

e

| 4 |
| 3 |
| 2 |
| 1 |
| 0 |
| –1 |
| –2 |
| –3 |
| –4 |

Let's play   A game for 2

You need

a green counter, a yellow counter, a dice

- Place the counters at each end of the track.
- Take turns to roll the dice.
- The yellow counter moves down the track and the green counter moves up the track.
- Record each number you land on.
- The winner is the player who reaches the other end of the track first.

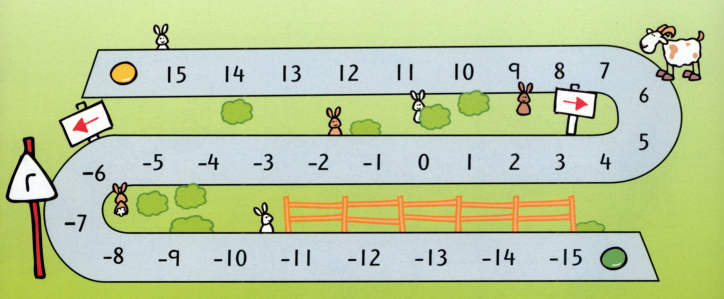

Let's practise

1 Copy and complete.

a $\frac{1}{8} = 1 \div \square$

b $\frac{1}{3} = \square \div 3$

c $\frac{\square}{5} = 1 \div 5$

d $\frac{1}{\square} = 1 \div 10$

e $\frac{1}{2} = \square \div \square$

f $\frac{\square}{\square} = \square \div \square$

Let's investigate

2 Jas draws two squares to show eighths.
Copy what Jas did.

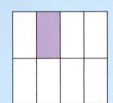 $\frac{1}{8} = 1 \div 8$

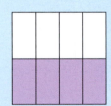 $\frac{4}{8} = 4 \div 8$

a Draw squares to show different numbers of eighths coloured.
Write a fraction and a matching division for each square.

b Write your fractions and division statements in order.
Start with the smallest.
Write about any patterns you can see.

c Jas sees that $\frac{4}{8}$ is equivalent to $\frac{1}{2}$.

He writes $\frac{4}{8} = 4 \div 8 = \frac{1}{2}$

Rewrite some of your statements giving
equivalent fractions.

? What if your squares showed tenths?

Let's practise

1 **a** $\frac{1}{2} = 1 \div \square$

b $1 \div 3 = \dfrac{\square}{\square}$

c $\square \div 10 = \dfrac{1}{\square}$

d $\frac{2}{3} = \square \div 3$

e $\dfrac{\square}{\square} = 3 \div 4$

f $3 \div \square = \dfrac{\square}{10}$

2 **a** $\frac{1}{2}$ of 30 = $\square$

b $\frac{1}{4}$ of 36 = $\square$

c $\frac{1}{3}$ of 24 = $\square$

Let's solve problems

3 The toyshop has 100 toy lorries.
Work out how many each child buys.

a Laura buys one tenth.

b Jack buys $\frac{1}{4}$.

c Mark buys $\frac{1}{10}$.

d Vicky buys one half.

e How many lorries does
the toyshop have left?

Let's investigate

4 **a** Between them Laura and Jack buy 8 toy animals.
Investigate what fraction of the 8 animals each could buy.

b Between them Laura, Jack and Vicky buy 12 toy cars.
Investigate what fraction of the 12 cars each could buy.

c Between them Laura, Jack, Vicky and Mark buy 10
video games.
Investigate what fraction each could buy.

Let's practise

1 Write the fraction.

a $\dfrac{\square}{4}$ is shaded

$\dfrac{1}{\square}$ is not shaded

b $\dfrac{1}{\square}$ is shaded

$\dfrac{\square}{3}$ is not shaded

c $\dfrac{3}{\square}$ is shaded

$\dfrac{\square}{8}$ is not shaded

d $\dfrac{\square}{\square}$ is shaded

$\dfrac{\square}{\square}$ is not shaded

2 Copy and complete.

a one third = $\dfrac{1}{3}$

two thirds = $\dfrac{\square}{3}$

three thirds = $\dfrac{\square}{3}$ = 1

four thirds = $\dfrac{\square}{3}$ = 1$\dfrac{\square}{3}$

five thirds = $\dfrac{\square}{\square}$ = 1$\dfrac{\square}{\square}$

b two quarters = $\dfrac{2}{4}$

three quarters = $\dfrac{\square}{4}$

four quarters = $\dfrac{\square}{\square}$ = 1

five quarters = $\dfrac{\square}{\square}$ = 1$\dfrac{\square}{4}$

six quarters = $\dfrac{\square}{\square}$ = 1$\dfrac{\square}{\square}$

Let's investigate

3

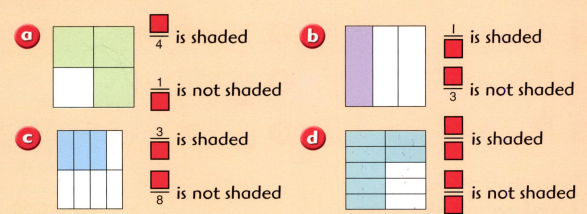

1 2 3 $\dfrac{1}{2}$ $\dfrac{3}{4}$ $\dfrac{7}{10}$

a Make as many mixed numbers as you can using the whole numbers and the fractions in the submarines.

b Which three mixed numbers are greater than 2 and less than 3?

c Which two mixed numbers are between 1$\dfrac{1}{2}$ and 2?

A mixed number is made from a whole number and a fraction.

Let's practise

1 Copy and complete.

a $\frac{5}{4}$ = 5 _____

b $\frac{3}{2}$ = ☐ halves

c $\frac{☐}{6}$ = 7 sixths

d $\frac{11}{☐}$ = 11 tenths

e $\frac{☐}{3}$ = 8 _____

f $\frac{12}{☐}$ = ☐ fifths

Let's solve problems

2 **a** The Hexagon Truck Company has a logo of 2 hexagons on each of its 12 trucks.

This is truck Number 8.

How many hexagons are coloured?
How many hexagons will be coloured on truck Number 11?

b The Circle Truck Company has a logo of 3 circles on each of its 12 trucks.

This is truck Number 9.

How many circles are coloured?
How many circles will be coloured on truck Number 5?

Let's investigate

3 Design a logo for the Square Truck Company which has 16 trucks and squares for its logo.
Colour your logo for truck Number 13.
How many squares have you coloured?

Let's practise

1 Copy and continue the pattern as far as you can.

> one tenth = $\frac{1}{10}$ = 0·1 = zero point one
>
> two tenths = $\frac{2}{10}$ = 0·2 = zero point two

2 Suzanne and Nicole timed toy cars rolling down a slope.

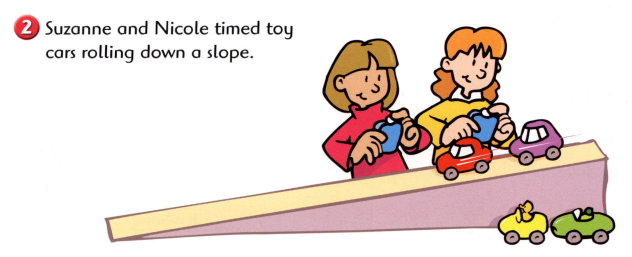

They wrote their results in words.

> The yellow car took six and four tenths of a second.
> The red car took three and nine tenths of a second.
> The green car took five and seven tenths of a second.
> The purple car took four and five tenths of a second.

Write each time as a decimal number in figures.

Let's investigate

3 Altogether, the 4 cars cost £4·40 at the toyshop.
What could be the price of each car?

4 If the 2 fastest cars cost £1·60 each,
what could the other 2 cars cost?

Let's practise

1 Copy and complete.

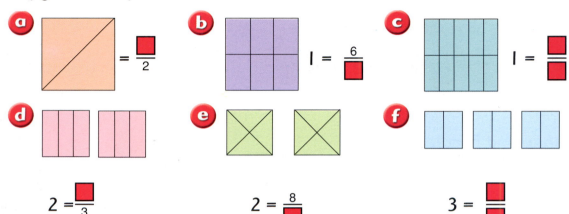

a $\square = \dfrac{\square}{2}$

b $1 = \dfrac{6}{\square}$

c $1 = \dfrac{\square}{\square}$

d $2 = \dfrac{\square}{3}$

e $2 = \dfrac{8}{\square}$

f $3 = \dfrac{\square}{\square}$

2 Use the equivalent fraction wall to copy and complete.

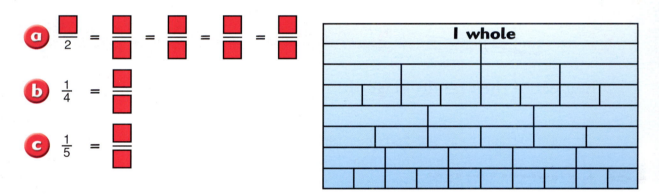

a $\dfrac{\square}{2} = \dfrac{\square}{\square} = \dfrac{\square}{\square} = \dfrac{\square}{\square} = \dfrac{\square}{\square}$

b $\dfrac{1}{4} = \dfrac{\square}{\square}$

c $\dfrac{1}{5} = \dfrac{\square}{\square}$

I whole	

Let's investigate

3 Find as many fractions as you can where the top and bottom numbers have a sum of 6.

Write an equivalent fraction for each one.

Write the fractions in order.

? What if the difference between the top and bottom number was 1?

Let's practise

1 Copy and complete.

a $\dfrac{4}{\square} = \dfrac{2}{\square} = \dfrac{1}{\square}$

b $\dfrac{\square}{6} = \dfrac{\square}{2}$

c $\dfrac{\square}{10} = \dfrac{1}{\square}$

d $\dfrac{6}{\square} = \dfrac{\square}{6} = \dfrac{\square}{\square}$

e $\dfrac{\square}{12} = \dfrac{2}{\square} = \dfrac{\square}{\square}$

f $\dfrac{\square}{\square} = \dfrac{\square}{\square} = \dfrac{\square}{\square}$

2 Copy and complete.

a $\dfrac{1}{2} + \dfrac{\square}{2} = 1$

b $\dfrac{\square}{3} + \dfrac{\square}{3} = 1$

c $\dfrac{1}{\square} + \dfrac{5}{6} = 1$

d $\dfrac{1}{2} + \dfrac{\square}{10} = 1$

e $\dfrac{3}{\square} + \dfrac{1}{\square} = 1$

f $\dfrac{\square}{8} + \dfrac{\square}{4} = 1$

Let's investigate

3 a Find two fractions that total 1.
Do this four times.

b Find three fractions that total 1.
Do this three times.

c Find four fractions that total 1.
Do this twice.

? What if the fractions total 2?

Let's practise

1 Copy and complete.

a $\frac{3}{10}$ = ☐ · ☐

b $\frac{9}{10}$ = ☐ · ☐

c $\frac{☐}{☐}$ = 0·7

d $\frac{1}{2}$ = ☐ · ☐

e $\frac{☐}{5}$ = ☐ · ☐

f $\frac{3}{4}$ = ☐ · ☐ ☐

Let's play   A game for 2

- Start at 'S'.

- Take turns to throw the dice and move your counter.

- If you land on a number, work out that fraction of 100. Colour that number of squares on your 100-square.

- The first to colour their whole 100-square is the winner.

You need

a 100-square each, coloured pencils, 1 dice, 2 counters

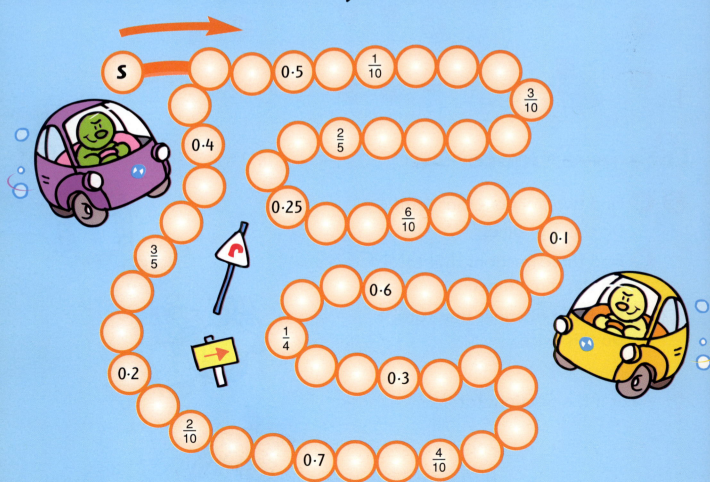

Let's practise

1 Write the fraction of each square you think is coloured.

a   b   c   d   e   f

Now write your answers in order, starting with the smallest.

2 Match the letters on the number line with the fractions in the box.

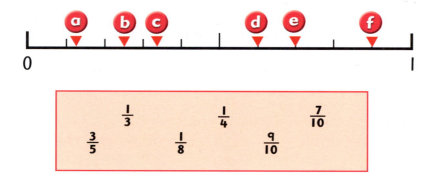

a   b   c   d   e   f

0   I

$\frac{1}{3}$ $\frac{1}{4}$ $\frac{7}{10}$

$\frac{3}{5}$ $\frac{1}{8}$ $\frac{9}{10}$

Let's solve problems

3

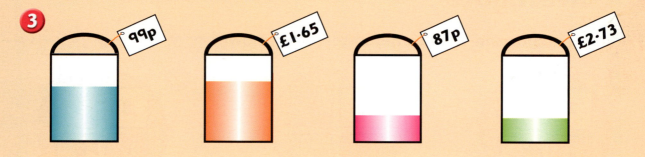

99p   £1·65   87p   £2·73

a Which colour has the most paint left?

b Which colour has the least paint left?

c Write the fraction of paint you think has been used from each tin.

d Now write your answers to part c in order of size,
starting with the largest.

e Each tin of paint was paid for using £1 coins.
How many £1 coins were used to pay for each colour?

Let's practise

1 **a**   64 + 35 = ☐

35 + 64 = ☐

b   28 + 53 = ☐

53 + 28 = ☐

c   47 + 19 = ☐

19 + 47 = ☐

What do you notice about each pair of answers? Explain why.

Let's solve problems

2 Jon bought these for his coach journey.

 **76p**   **64p**   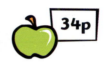 **34p**    **23p**

What is the cost of

a   the hat and the drink

b   the drink and the hat

c   the apple and the pen

d   the pen and the apple?

Let's investigate

3 Add the numbers in each target in the order shown.

a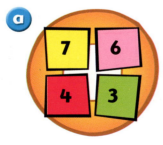

| 7 | 6 |
| 4 | 3 |

b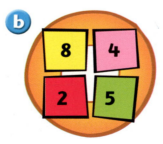

| 8 | 4 |
| 2 | 5 |

c

| 8 | 7 |
| 6 | 9 |

☐ + ☐ + ☐ + ☐ = ☐   ☐ + ☐ + ☐ + ☐ = ☐   ☐ + ☐ + ☐ + ☐ = ☐

☐ + ☐ + ☐ + ☐ = ☐   ☐ + ☐ + ☐ + ☐ = ☐   ☐ + ☐ + ☐ + ☐ = ☐

☐ + ☐ + ☐ + ☐ = ☐   ☐ + ☐ + ☐ + ☐ = ☐   ☐ + ☐ + ☐ + ☐ = ☐

☐ + ☐ + ☐ + ☐ = ☐   ☐ + ☐ + ☐ + ☐ = ☐   ☐ + ☐ + ☐ + ☐ = ☐

d Write some hints about how to add several numbers quickly.

Let's practise

① Follow each train to find the answer.

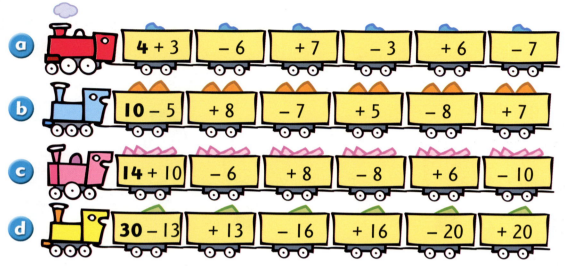

a $4 + 3$ $- 6$ $+ 7$ $- 3$ $+ 6$ $- 7$

b $10 - 5$ $+ 8$ $- 7$ $+ 5$ $- 8$ $+ 7$

c $14 + 10$ $- 6$ $+ 8$ $- 8$ $+ 6$ $- 10$

d $30 - 13$ $+ 13$ $- 16$ $+ 16$ $- 20$ $+ 20$

What do you notice? Explain why.

Let's investigate

② Use these facts to help you answer the questions below.

$27 + 8 = 35$

$17 - 9 = 8$

$27 + 19 = 46$

$32 - 18 = 14$

$16 + 25 = 41$

$38 - 29 = 9$

a $41 - 25 = \square$

b $8 + 9 = \square$

c $18 + 14 = \square$

d $9 + 29 = \square$

e $46 - 27 = \square$

f $35 - 27 = \square$

③ Write 5 other pairs of addition and subtraction facts that have the same 3 numbers.

$8 + 26 = 34$ and $34 - 8 = 26$

④ Find 3 numbers in the box to make 2 additions and 2 subtractions. Investigate doing this as many ways as you can.

61	88	34
27	91	30

Let's practise

1 **a** $9 + 5 = \square$ **b** $6 + 8 = \square$ **c** $7 + 11 = \square$

     d $15 - 7 = \square$ **e** $16 - 9 = \square$ **f** $20 - 13 = \square$

2 Add or subtract 2 numbers from the balloons to make the number in the question.

 17    8    9    7    20    12

a 15   **b** 5   **c** 11   **d** 16   **e** 13   **f** 19

Let's play   A game for 2

- Place the cards face down in a pile.
- Take turns to turn over 2 cards.
- Find the difference between them.
- The first player to say the answer scores 1 point.
- The first to score 10 points wins.

> **You need**
> cards for numbers 1 to 20

Let's investigate

> **You need**
> digit cards for numbers 0 to 9

3 **a** Use all 10 cards to make 5 pairs of additions, all with different answers.
Find different ways of doing this.

     b Use all 10 cards to make 5 pairs of additions, all with the **same** answer.
Can you find different ways of doing this?

? What if you use the cards to make subtractions?

Let's practise

1. **a** 59 + ☐ = 100   **b** ☐ + 83 = 100   **c** ☐ + 44 = 100
   d 38 + ☐ = 100   **e** 72 + ☐ = 100   **f** ☐ + 47 = 100

Let's play   A game for 2

You need
a counter each, a dice

- Take turns to roll the dice and move the counter in any direction.
- When you land on a number, write **both** the number **and** the number that adds to it to make 100.
- Your partner checks your answer. Score a point if you are correct.
- The first to score 10 points is the winner.

Let's investigate

You need   digit cards for numbers 1 to 9

2. Investigate ways of using 4 cards to make additions that total 100.

3 8 + 6 2 = 100

Let's practise

1 Write the number to add to make 1000.

a 300   **b** 450   **c** 950

d 700   **e** 250   **f** 800

g 150   **h** 400   **i** 650

Let's solve problems

2 There were 1000 people at the airport.

a If 750 of them were children, how many were adults?

b If 350 had luggage, how many had no luggage?

c If 150 were going to Greece, how many were not going to Greece?

Let's play   A game for 2

- Spread the cards out face down.

- Take turns to pick 2 cards.

- Add the numbers together.
  If they total 1000, keep the cards.
  If not, put them back, face down.

- The player with more cards at the end is the winner.

> **You need**
>
> 19 cards marked 50, 100, 150, 200, 250, ... 950 and an extra 500 card

Let's investigate

3 Investigate making 1000 with three number cards.

> **You need**
>
> the number cards from the game above

Let's practise

1 **a** 19 + 19 = ☐ **b** 23 + 23 = ☐ **c** 34 + 34 = ☐
d 160 + 160 = ☐ **e** 180 + 180 = ☐ **f** 210 + 210 = ☐

2 ● Choose a number in the wall.
● Double the number.
● Now add 1 to the number and subtract 1 from the number.
● Write your answers like this.

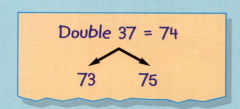

Double 37 = 74

73   75

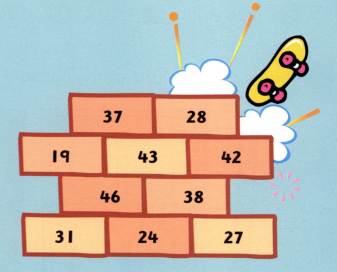

37	28
19	43	42
46	38
31	24	27

● Do this for all the numbers in the wall.

3 Use your answers to question 2 to solve these 'near doubles'.

a 37 + 36 = **b** 28 + 27 = **c** 24 + 25 =
d 19 + 18 = **e** 46 + 45 = **f** 370 + 360 =
g 280 + 290 = **h** 310 + 320 = **i** 470 + 460 =

Let's solve problems

4 **a** Paula's mum is 1 year older than Paula's dad.
The total of their ages is 77.
How old is Paula's mum?

b Dev scored 10 more than Sam.
The total of their scores was 470.
How many did Sam score?

Let's practise

1 **a** 43 + 39 = ☐   **b** 45 + 31 = ☐   **c** 93 + 9 = ☐

   d 63 + 21 = ☐   **e** 94 + 19 = ☐   **f** 157 − 9 = ☐

   g 206 − 11 = ☐   **h** 505 − 19 = ☐   **i** 708 − 21 = ☐

2 Choose a bottle from each cupboard to make a question.

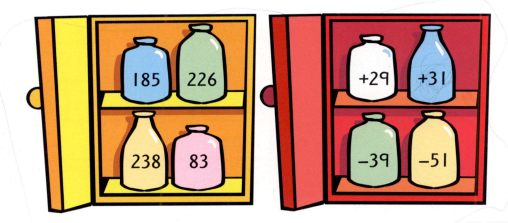

185 + 29 = 185 + 30 − 1 = 214

Do this in 16 different ways. How many different answers are there?

Let's investigate

3 Add or subtract 2 numbers from the wheels to make the frame number.

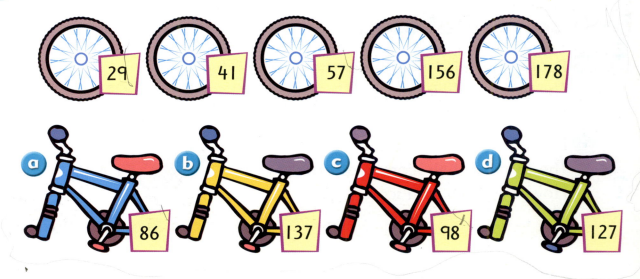

Let's practise

1 **a** 60 + 30 + 20 = ☐

b 70 + 10 + 90 = ☐

c 40 + 80 + 60 = ☐

d 90 + 50 + ☐ = 170

e 20 + ☐ + 70 = 170

f ☐ + 60 + 50 = 170

Let's solve problems

2 **a** Alice has 4 money boxes in which she has £8, £11, £9 and £19. How much does she have altogether?

b In Key Stage 2 classes there are 120 children altogether. In Year 3 there are 28 children, in Year 4 there are 27 and in Year 5 there are 31. How many children are in Year 6?

c 53 tickets are sold on Monday, 71 on Tuesday and 88 on Wednesday. How many have been sold so far?

d Sol has 240 stamps in one album and 270 in another. How many stamps does he have altogether?

Let's investigate

3 **a** Investigate finding 3 different multiples of 10 with a total of 100.

b Investigate finding 4 different multiples of 10.

c Investigate finding 5 different multiples of 10.

💡 What if the numbers were multiples of 100 with a total of 1000?

Let's practise

1 Count up to find the difference.

+ 4   + 3

496   500   503

503 − 496 → 496 + 4 + 3 = 503

a 502 − 497 = ☐   b 506 − 493 = ☐   c 508 − 492 = ☐

d 606 − 594 = ☐   e 607 − 598 = ☐   f 609 − 591 = ☐

2 Use the counting-up method to find the answer.

+ 7   + 4

4993   5000   5004

5004 − 4993 → 4993 + 7 + 4 = 5004

a 5006 − 4999 = ☐   b 5002 − 4994 = ☐   c 4003 − 3996 = ☐

d 5008 − 4991 = ☐   e 7007 − 6992 = ☐   f 8005 − 7993 = ☐

Let's solve problems

3 a On Monday there were 788 cars in the car park.
On Tuesday there were 806. How many more were there on
Tuesday than on Monday?

b Yesterday there were 1002 cars in the car park.
Today there are 974. How many more were there yesterday?

c The difference between the number of cars on Thursday and
Friday was 6. On Thursday there were 1997. How many could
there have been on Friday?

Let's practise

    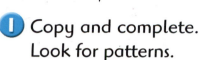 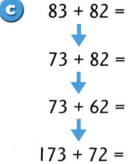

1 Copy and complete.
Look for patterns.

a
97 + 14 =
↓
97 + 15 =
↓
107 + 15 =
↓
107 + 115 =

b
56 + 29 =
↓
66 + 29 =
↓
66 + 39 =
↓
166 + 139 =

c
83 + 82 =
↓
73 + 82 =
↓
73 + 62 =
↓
173 + 72 =

2 Copy and complete.
Look for patterns.

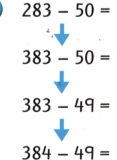

a
111 − 14 =
↓
111 − 15 =
↓
121 − 15 =
↓
121 − 35 =

b
207 − 29 =
↓
217 − 29 =
↓
217 − 39 =
↓
317 − 39 =

c
283 − 50 =
↓
383 − 50 =
↓
383 − 49 =
↓
384 − 49 =

Let's investigate

321 + 88 = 409
341 + ? = 409

3 Investigate additions of 3-digit and 2-digit
numbers that have the answer 409.

 What if 2-digit numbers were subtracted from
3-digit numbers and the answer was still 409?

Let's practise

1 **a** $62 + \square = 82$ **b** $34 + \square = 74$ **c** $21 + \square = 61$

    d $\square + 60 = 95$ **e** $\square + 50 = 87$ **f** $\square + 70 = 98$

2 **a** $29 + \square = 100$ **b** $57 + \square = 100$ **c** $48 + \square = 100$

    d $\square + 63 = 100$ **e** $\square + 11 = 100$ **f** $\square + 36 = 100$

3 **a** $78 - \square = 28$ **b** $51 - \square = 21$ **c** $39 - \square = 19$

    d $\square - 20 = 62$ **e** $\square - 50 = 17$ **f** $\square - 40 = 35$

Let's investigate

You need

digit cards for numbers 0 to 9

4 ● Choose 3 digit cards.

● Make as many 3-digit numbers as you can.

a Which of your numbers has the greatest difference between it and the next multiple of 100?

b Which of your numbers has the smallest difference between it and the next multiple of 100?

What if you chose four digit cards, made 4-digit numbers and found the difference between them and the next multiple of 1000?

Let's practise

1 **a** 45 + 55 + 30 = ☐   **b** 28 + 32 + 45 = ☐   **c** 30 + 55 + 25 = ☐

d 49 + 50 + 21 = ☐   **e** 57 + 23 + 60 = ☐   **f** 44 + 45 + 80 = ☐

2 **a** 61 + ☐ + 35 = 154   **b** 48 + ☐ + 56 = 178

c 72 + ☐ + 69 = 234   **d** 85 + ☐ + 71 = 243

3 Use the digits in the balloon to make 2-digit numbers.
Complete the number sentences below.
Use each digit once only in a number sentence.

a ☐ + ☐ = 126   **b** ☐ + ☐ + ☐ = 157

c ☐ + ☐ + ☐ = 176   **d** ☐ + ☐ + ☐ = 120

Let's investigate

4 Use only the digits 5, 5, 5, 3, 3, 3 to write additions
of two or three 2-digit numbers.

Let's practise

1 **a** 328 + 40 = ☐   **b** 583 – 40 = ☐   **c** 347 + 40 = ☐
   d 844 – 50 = ☐   **e** 977 + 50 = ☐   **f** 525 – 50 = ☐

2 ● Choose 4 of these cards to make a question.

● Write it down.

● Find the answer by counting on or back.

Do this as many times as you can.

493 + 40 = 533

703	
500	=
40	300	60
–	+	493	376

Let's investigate

You need
cards for digits 0–8
and one extra 0 card

3 Digits are missing from the addition and the subtraction below.

   +      –   ☐ ☐ 0

● Use your cards to complete the addition and subtraction.
● Write them down and find the answers.
Do this 6 times.

a Which addition has the greatest answer?

b Which subtraction has the smallest answer?

c Investigate making an addition and a subtraction so that the answer is greater for the addition than for the subtraction.

How many ways can you find?

Let's practise

1 Ben's cat has walked across his work.
Copy and complete each addition to make it correct.

a
```
    5 2 7
  +   5 4
    5 0 0
      7 0
      1 1
    5
```

b
```
    4 5 4
  +   3 9
    4 0 0
      8 0
      1
    4
```

c
```
    3 2 6
  +   4 5
    3 0 0
      6 0
        1
      7 1
```

d
```
    7 4 3
  + 1 8 6
    8 0 0
    1 2
        9
    9
```

e
```
    3 7 8
  + 5 4 3
    8 0 0
    1
    9 2 1
```

f
```
    6 0 5
  + 1 3 8
      0 0
      3 0
    7
```

g
```
    5 4 9
  + 2 5
    7 0
      9 0
      1 6
    8
```

h
```
    6 5 4
  + 2 7 9
    8
    1
      1 3
    9 3
```

Let's solve problems

2 Which 2 money boxes would you need to buy each cat basket?

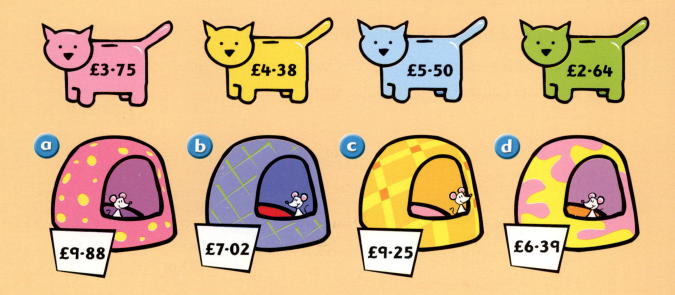

£3·75   £4·38   £5·50   £2·64

a £9·88   **b** £7·02   **c** £9·25   **d** £6·39

Let's practise

1 Copy and complete.

a
```
    2 5 3
  +   3 4
  _____
```

b
```
      6 1
  + 3 3 8
  _____
```

c
```
    2 5 6
  + 4 3 9
  _____
```

d
```
    7 0 6
  + 2 7 8
  _____
```

e
```
    3 5 7
  + 3 8 4
  _____
```

f
```
    8 1 5
  + 1 6 6
  _____
```

2 Add 3 of the numbers on the lorries to find each total.

a 788   **b** 577   **c** 450   **d** 783

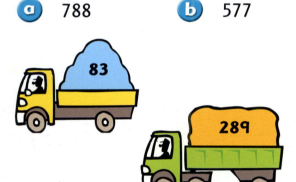

Let's solve problems

3 Joe drives to 3 towns, one after the other.

a Make a list of all the different ways he could go.

b How far would each journey be?

Joe is here!

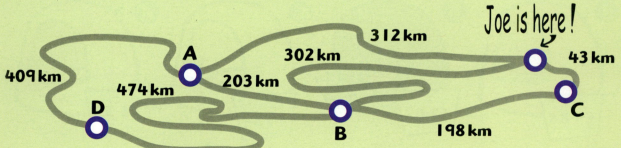

409 km   474 km   203 km   302 km   312 km   43 km   198 km

D   A   B   C

Let's practise

1 Find the total of each pair of prices.

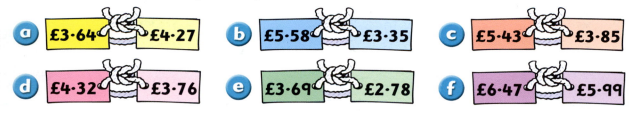

a £3·64   £4·27   b £5·58   £3·35   c £5·43   £3·85

d £4·32   £3·76   e £3·69   £2·78   f £6·47   £5·99

Let's solve problems

2 Each person buys 2 items.
Which 2 items did each person buy?
Write your answer as an addition.

£2·52   £8·27   £3·75   £3·24   £8·42   £6·03   £6·50

a Ian spent £5·76.   b Sally spent £10·25.
c Jan spent £14·30.   d Raz spent £14·92.
e Poppy spent £9·27.   f Olly spent £6·99.

Let's practise

Aysha uses this method for subtraction.

```
   5 3 6   =   5 0 0 + 3 0 + 6   =   5 0 0 + 2 0 + 1 6
 -   5 7   -           5 0 + 7   -           5 0 +  7

                                  =   4 0 0 + 1 2 0 + 1 6
                                  -               5 0 +  7
                                      4 0 0 +   7 0 +  9

                                      Answer   4 7 9
```

Her friend Sufia uses a shorter method.

```
   5 3 6   =   5 2 ⁶ 6   =   4 ¹2 ⁶ 6
 -   5 7   -     5 7     -       5 7

                Answer   4 7 9
```

I'll adjust from tens to units first and then from hundreds to tens.

1 Try one of these methods to find the answers.

   a   671 – 54   **b**   756 – 45   **c**   574 – 86

   d   762 – 94   **e**   637 – 485   **f**   709 – 573

Now check your answers by adding.

2 Copy and complete this diagram.
Write the differences along each line.

This shows the difference
between 994 and 723.

```
 994
-723
 271
```

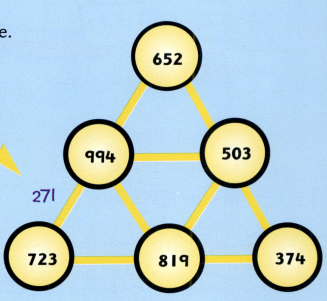

652

994   503

271

723   819   374

Let's practise

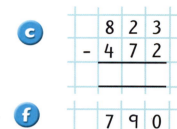

1 Copy and complete.

a
```
    5 1 8
 -    7 5
 ─────────
```

b
```
    4 3 2
 -    5 1
 ─────────
```

c
```
    8 2 3
 -  4 7 2
 ─────────
```

d
```
    7 3 3
 -  4 5 8
 ─────────
```

e
```
    3 0 7
 -  2 6 9
 ─────────
```

f
```
    7 9 0
 -  6 9 5
 ─────────
```

Let's solve problems

2

Travel Shop
Flights to | Cost
Paris | £94
Singapore | £429
Perth | £617
Hong Kong | £380
Rome | £183
Sydney | £752
Wellington | £789

Getaways
Flights to.....Cost
Paris...........£127
Singapore....£391
Perth...........£469
Hong Kong..£512
Rome...........£301
Sydney.........£599
Wellington...£907

- Compare the cost of flights to the same city. Which is cheaper? By how much?

- Record your answers in a table like this.

- Use a suitable to check your answers.

City	Better price		Difference
	Travelshop	Getaways	
Paris	✔		£33
Singapore			

Let's investigate

3 Take three digits from each suitcase to make two 3-digit numbers.
Find the difference between them.
Investigate finding the greatest and least differences.

Let's practise

1 How much will be left in each purse if you buy the item shown?

a   £5·16   £2·74

b   £7·47   £5·92

c   £6·23   £4·15

d   £4·09   £2·28

e   £7·99   £3·48

f   £6·20   £4·07

Let's solve problems

2 Pair these prices so that the difference between the prices in each pair is £1·87.

£8·29

£5·09

£7·49

£7·39

£9·26

£9·36

£6·96

£6·42

3 Jo was given 2 amounts of money on her birthday.
The difference between them was £1·40 and their total was £3·60.
What were the amounts of money?

Let's practise

1 Which of the 3 numbers is most likely to be the answer?
Show how you made your estimate.

342 – 198
76   166
(144)

> I think 144 is the answer. I rounded each number to the nearest 10 to make 340 – 200 = 140.

a 541 + 367

808   848
908

b 358 + 409

767   807
827

c 412 – 258

136   154
206

d 573 – 164

351   409
459

e 289 + 467

706   724
756

f 538 + 196

704   734
774

Let's investigate

2 Katie rounded a subtraction to 650 – 200 = 450
Write 6 possibilities for Katie's subtraction.
Find the correct answer to each one.

 What if Katie had rounded an addition to 540 + 330?

Let's practise

1 Rob has done his homework.

A 147 + 42 = 189	G 373 − 62 = 311
B 527 + 65 = 582	H 476 − 49 = 427
C 324 + 237 = 561	I 682 − 391 = 391
D 753 + 165 = 918	J 715 − 508 = 207
E 627 + 283 = 900	K 812 − 357 = 455
F 295 + 406 = 701	L 666 − 478 = 178

a Check each addition with a subtraction.
Which of Rob's sums are correct?

b Check each subtraction with an addition.
What mistakes has Rob made?

Let's investigate

2 a Use 3-digit numbers only.
Write 6 additions with the
answer 601. Check each one
using the inverse operation.

100 + 501 = 601   Check: 601 − 100 = 501

b Look at each addition again.
Do another check using an equivalent
calculation or what you know about
the sums of odd and even numbers.

? What if you subtracted 3-digit numbers
to get the answer 601?

Let's practise

1.
a $3 \times 7 = \square$ **b** $4 \times 6 = \square$ **c** $3 \times 9 = \square$

d $5 \times 7 = \square$ **e** $3 \times 5 = \square$ **f** $5 \times 8 = \square$

2. Copy and complete.

a $\square \div 5 = 4$ **b** $\square \div 6 = 3$ **c** $\square \div 7 = 2$

d $\square \div 3 = 8$ **e** $\square \div 8 = 4$ **f** $\square \div 4 = 9$

3. Copy and complete.   Example:

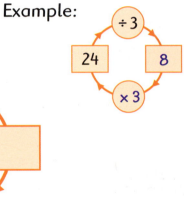

a

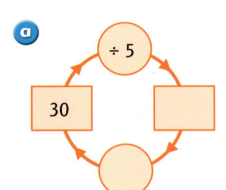

b

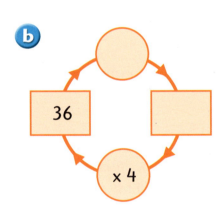

Let's investigate

4. Use the cards to make as many correct number statements as you can.

3 4 5 6

12 15 18 20 24 30

Let's practise

1 Copy each pair.
Write whether the answers are the same or different.
If the answers are different, write what they are.

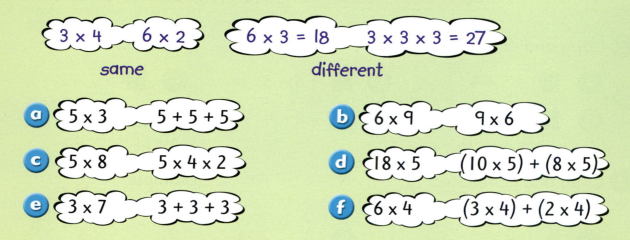

3×4 6×2 $6 \times 3 = 18$ $3 \times 3 \times 3 = 27$

same   different

a 5×3 $5 + 5 + 5$ **b** 6×9 9×6

c 5×8 $5 \times 4 \times 2$ **d** 18×5 $(10 \times 5) + (8 \times 5)$

e 3×7 $3 + 3 + 3$ **f** 6×4 $(3 \times 4) + (2 \times 4)$

2 Here are three ways of calculating 24×5.

I know that
24 multiplied by 10 is 240
and half of 240 is 120.

I multiplied 20
by 5 to get 100 and
then 4 by 5 to get 20.
The answer is 120.

a Which way do you like best? Why?

b Which way do you like least? Why?

c How could you calculate 18×6?

I know that
$6 \times 5 = 30$, so 12×5
must be 60 and 24×5
must be 120.

Let's investigate

3 Write as many multiplications as you can for each number.

a 6×4 24   **b** 18   **c** 30

$2 \times 2 \times 2 \times 3$

Let's practise

1 Copy and complete these number trails by doubling.

a 7 → 14 → ☐ → ☐

b 6 → ☐ → ☐ → ☐

c 11 → ☐ → ☐ → ☐

d 9 → ☐ → ☐ → ☐

2 Copy and complete these number trails by halving.

a 48 → 24 → ☐ → ☐

b 64 → ☐ → ☐ → ☐

c 96 → ☐ → ☐ → ☐

d 160 → ☐ → ☐ → ☐

3 Copy and complete.
Find the answer to each multiplication.
What do you notice?

a
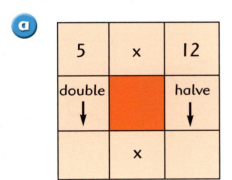

5	×	12
double ↓		halve ↓
	×	

b
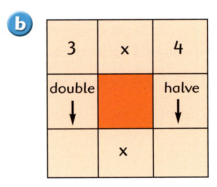

3	×	4
double ↓		halve ↓
	×	

Let's investigate

4 Calum started with 24 and kept halving.

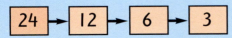

24 → 12 → 6 → 3

He stopped after halving 3 times
as he had reached an odd number.
He called it a 3-link chain.
Find the longest chain that starts with a 2-digit number.

Let's practise

1 Copy and complete.

    a ☐ × ☐ = 30   **b** ☐ × ☐ = 32   **c** ☐ × ☐ = 25

    d ☐ × ☐ = 40   **e** ☐ × ☐ = 36   **f** ☐ × ☐ = 72

2 Write a list of the numbers from 30 to 40.
Divide each one by 3, by 4 and by 5.
Write each division sentence.

$30 ÷ 3 = 10$, $30 ÷ 4 = 7 \text{ r } 2$, $30 ÷ 5 = 6$

3 How many £3 tickets can you buy for £29?
How much money will be left?

$29 ÷ 3 = 9 \text{ r } 2$

9 tickets   £2 left over

    a How many £3 tickets for £26?

    b How many £4 tickets for £29?

    c How many £5 tickets for £33?

Let's investigate

4 Investigate using 3 of the cards to
make divisions which have
answers with a remainder of 1.

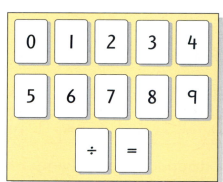

    [2] [5] ÷ [8] =

? What if the remainder was 2, 3, 4, ... 8, 9?

Let's practise

1. **a** $27 \div 5 = \square$ **b** $28 \div 3 = \square$ **c** $38 \div 4 = \square$ **d** $43 \div 5 = \square$
   e $41 \div 4 = \square$ **f** $39 \div 5 = \square$ **g** $52 \div 4 = \square$ **h** $47 \div 2 = \square$

Let's solve problems

£5
10 pages
6 photos on a page

2. How many albums can Phil buy if he has
   a £27 **b** £33?

3. How many photos can each album hold?

4. Phil has 34 photos to put in an album.
   a How many pages will he need?
   b How many pages will be full?

5. If he has 45 photos to put in an album, how many pages will he need?

6. Phil fills 5 pages of an album and has 3 photos left over.
   How many photos is that altogether?

7. He fills 6 pages of an album and has 2 photos left over.
   How many photos is that altogether?

Let's practise

① Write the calculations. Find the answers.

a 8

b 6

c 40

d 24

② Copy and complete these grids.

a

x	5	6	8
3	15		
0			
7			

b

x	3	8	
		72	
	12		28
7			

Let's play A game for 2

Take turns to:

● Choose a number from the grid.

● Say how many 4s make that number.

● Ask your partner to check your answer.

● If you are right, cover the number with a counter in your colour.

● The winner is the first to get 4 in a line in any direction.

24	32	4	20	28
8	36	16	0	8
12	28	32	36	24
28	0	40	32	12
20	24	16	4	36

Let's practise

1 **a** 260 × 2   **b** Twice 480   **c** Double 360

    d 270 + 270   **e** 2 × 390   **f** 470 doubled

Check your answers by halving.

2 Find half of each price.

    a £820   **b** £960   **c** £1400   **d** £3800

    e £840   **f** £3500   **g** £4600   **h** £1200

Check your answers by doubling.

Let's play   A game for 2

You need

counters

Take turns to:

- Pick a number on the bus.

- Double it.
  Find your answer in the grid and put a counter on it.

- Do this with all the numbers on the bus.

What letter have you made?

80	820	940	3200	380
560	1800	220	110	780
210	340	140	500	200
1600	680	920	190	230
100	4600	120	130	710

Make a game like this of your own.

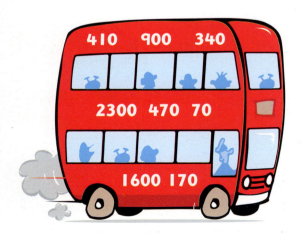

410   900   340

2300   470   70

1600   170

Let's practise

1 Multiply these numbers by 10, moving each digit 1 place to the left.

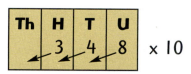

a 348 **b** 459 **c** 907 **d** 560 **e** 255 **f** 600

2 Multiply these numbers by 100, moving each digit 2 places to the left.

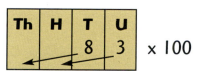

a 83 **b** 273 **c** 827 **d** 904 **e** 390 **f** 500

Let's solve problems

3 a Iain earns £32 per day. How much will he earn in 10 days?

  b Sally earns £47 per day. How much will she earn in 10 days?

  c Deepa earns £69 per day. How much will she earn in 100 days?

  d Frank earns £74 per day. How much will he earn in 100 days?

Sally   Iain   Deepa   Frank

4 Beth earns 10 times more than Bob.
Bill earns 10 times more than Beth.
In 1 hour they earn £444 altogether.
How much does each earn?

What if Bob earns £5, Beth earns 9 times more than Bob and
Bill earns 9 times more than Beth?

Let's practise

1 Use doubling or halving to complete these questions.

a 8 x 20 = ☐   **b** 13 x 20 = ☐   **c** 27 x 20 = ☐

d 12 x 5 = ☐   **e** 46 x 5 = ☐   **f** 15 x 4 = ☐

g 33 x 4 = ☐   **h** 32 ÷ 4 = ☐   **i** 9 ÷ 4 = ☐

Let's solve problems

2 a Molly collects £24 for charity. Niall collects twice as much as Molly. Ollie collects double Niall's amount. How much money altogether?

b Bruce has 42 monster cards. Alice has half as many cards as Bruce. Catherine has twice as many cards as Bruce. How many cards does each of them have?

Lets investigate

3 Salmi starts with 3 x 2 = 6 and doubles numbers in turn to make new multiplications.

3 x 2 = 6   6 x 4 = 24   12 x 8 = 96   24 x 16 = 384

3 x 4 = 12   6 x 8 = 48   12 x 16 = 192

Start with 2 x 5 = 10 and do what Salmi did.
Now choose your own starter multiplication.

Let's practise

1 Divide these numbers by 10, moving each digit 1 place to the right.

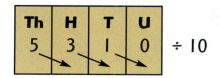

Th	H	T	U	
5	3	1	0	÷ 10

- **a** 30 ÷ 10
- **b** 570 ÷ 10
- **c** 640 ÷ 10
- **d** 900 ÷ 10
- **e** 8010 ÷ 10
- **f** 5000 ÷ 10
- **g** 18 200 ÷ 10
- **h** 20 650 ÷ 10
- **i** 82 000 ÷ 10

2 Divide these numbers by 100, moving each digit 2 places to the right.

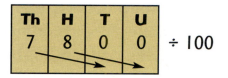

Th	H	T	U	
7	8	0	0	÷ 100

- **a** 9200 ÷ 100
- **b** 4300 ÷ 100
- **c** 6400 ÷ 100
- **d** 17 000 ÷ 100
- **e** 80 500 ÷ 100
- **f** 10 000 ÷ 100
- **g** 700 ÷ 100
- **h** 12 800 ÷ 100
- **i** 50 200 ÷ 100

Let's investigate

3 Choose 4 of these cards to make a correct number sentence.

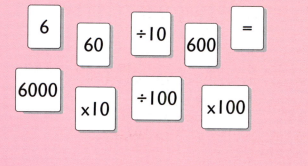

6   60   ÷10   600   =

6000   ×10   ÷100   ×100

6000 ÷100 = 60

James made 10 different number sentences. How many can you make?

Let's practise

1 Copy and complete.

a 13 x 5 = ☐ 　 **b** 14 x 3 = ☐ 　 **c** 16 x 4 = ☐ 　 **d** 22 x 5 = ☐

e 24 x 3 = ☐ 　 **f** 18 x 5 = ☐ 　 **g** 23 x 4 = ☐ 　 **h** 26 x 5 = ☐

Let's solve problems

2 Mr Tewin owns a sweet shop.

a He has 6 jars of fruit gums. How many fruit gums is that?

b He has 3 jars of toffees. How many toffees is that?

c He has 4 jars of mints. How many mints is that?

d On Saturday he shares out a whole jar of toffees between 3 children. How many toffees does each get?

e On Tuesday he shares out a whole jar of mints between 4 children. How many mints does each get?

f Mr Tewin has 5 full jars of fudge. He has a total of 200 pieces of fudge. How many pieces of fudge are in each jar?

g On Friday Mr Tewin only has $1\frac{1}{2}$ jars of fruit gums left. How many fruit gums is this?

Let's practise

Jack, Molly and Ali are multiplying. They each use a different method.

Jack's method

47 × 5

40 × 5 = 200

7 × 5 = __35__

200 + 35 = 235

Molly's method

47 × 5

50 × 5 = 250

3 × 5 = __15__

250 − 15 = 235

Ali's method

47 × 5

×	40	7
5	200	35

200 + 35 = 235

1 Answer each question and check using a different method.
Approximate first.

a 35 × 5

b 26 × 4

c 19 × 6

d 48 × 6

e 39 × 3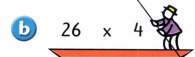

f 62 × 7

Let's play   A game for 1

- Turn over 2 cards and arrange them to make a 2-digit number.

The target is 300.

You need
digit cards for numbers 0 to 9, a dice

- Roll the dice.

- Multiply the number made by the cards by the number on the dice.
Show your method on paper.

8 1 ×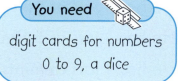

- How near to 300 is your answer?

- Do this 5 times.

Can you make 300 exactly?

81 × 4   80 × 4 = 320
                1 × 4 =   4
            320 + 4 = 324

Let's practise

1. Ben's cat has walked across his work.
Copy and complete each multiplication
to make it correct.

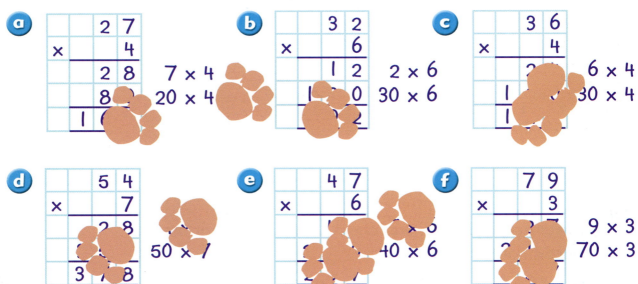

a
```
    2 7
×     4
    2 8    7 × 4
  8 ▨▨    20 × 4
1 ▨▨
```

b
```
    3 2
×     6
    1 2    2 × 6
1 ▨ 0    30 × 6
▨ ▨ 2
```

c
```
    3 6
×     4
  2 ▨▨    6 × 4
1 ▨▨    30 × 4
1 ▨
```

d
```
    5 4
×     7
  2 8 ▨
▨ ▨ ▨    50 × 7
3 ▨ 8
```

e
```
    4 7
×     6
  ▨ ▨ ▨
▨ ▨ ▨    40 × 6
```

f
```
    7 9
×     3
  ▨ ▨    9 × 3
▨ ▨    70 × 3
```

Let's investigate

2. Choose numbers from the wheel and multiply them
by 3 or 4 to make the numbers on the boards.

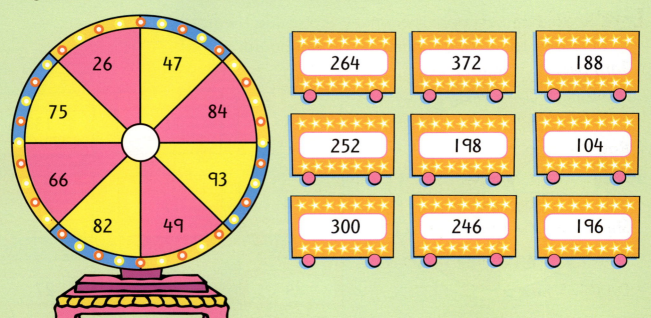

Wheel numbers: 26, 47, 75, 84, 66, 93, 82, 49

Boards: 264, 372, 188, 252, 198, 104, 300, 246, 196

Let's practise

Jack, Molly and Ali are dividing. They each use a different method.

Jack's method

$$75 ÷ 3$$

$$75 = 30 + 30 + 15$$

$$÷3 \quad ÷3 \quad ÷3$$

$$10 + 10 + 5$$

$$= 25$$

Molly's method

$$75 ÷ 3$$

$$= (60 + 15) ÷ 3$$

$$= 20 + 5$$

$$= 25$$

Ali's method

$$75 ÷ 3$$

$$75$$

$$- \ 60 \quad (20 × 3)$$

$$15$$

$$- \ 15 \quad (5 × 3)$$

$$0$$

$$= 25$$

1 Answer each question and check using a different method. Approximate first.

a 85 ÷ 5   **b** 51 ÷ 3   **c** 92 ÷ 4

d 96 ÷ 3   **e** 84 ÷ 4   **f** 78 ÷ 3

Let's investigate

2 Choose numbers from the wheel and divide them by 3 or 4 to make the numbers on the boards.

 26    28   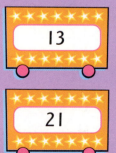 13

19   17   21

 24    23   27

Wheel numbers: 52, 81, 78, 76, 96, 68, 69, 84

Let's practise

1. Tanji's pet snail has crawled across her work.
   Copy and complete each division to make it correct.

a)
```
      1 9
  5 ) 9 6
  - 5 0     10 x 5
    4 6
  - 4 5     9 x 5
      1
```
Answer: r1

b)
```
  4 ) 6 3
  - 4 0     10 x 4
    2 3
            x 4
```
Answer.

c)
```
  6 ) 9 2
  - 6 0     x 6
            x 6
```
Answer.

d)
```
  5 ) 7 7
```
Answer:

e)
```
  3 ) 8 4
```
Answer:

f)
```
  4 ) 7 8
```
Answer:

Let's solve problems

2   **Miss Jones**

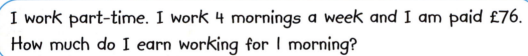

I work part-time. I work 4 mornings a week and I am paid £76.
How much do I earn working for 1 morning?

3   **Mr Li**

I work part-time. I work 6 evenings a week and I am paid £84.
How much do I earn working for 1 evening?

4   **Mrs Patel**

I work part-time. I work 3 afternoons a week and I am paid £78.
How much do I earn working for 1 afternoon?

Let's solve problems

Solve these problems.
Write about how you worked out each one.

1. Find 2 numbers

   a) with a sum of 4 and a difference of 4

   b) with a sum of 8 and a difference of 4

   c) with a total of 20 and a difference of 4

   d) with a total of 100 and a difference of 4.

$$\square + \triangle = 4$$
$$\square - \triangle = 4$$

2. Find 2 numbers

   a) with a sum of 10 and a product of 25

   b) with a sum of 10 and a product of 24

   c) with a sum of 10 and a product of 21

   d) with a sum of 10 and a product of 16.

$$\triangle + \square = 10$$
$$\triangle \times \square = 25$$

3. Find 3 numbers

   a) with a sum of 6 and a product of 6

   b) with a sum of 12 and a product of 48

   c) with a sum of 15 and a product of 105.

$$\triangle + \square + \diamond = 6$$
$$\triangle \times \square \times \diamond = 6$$

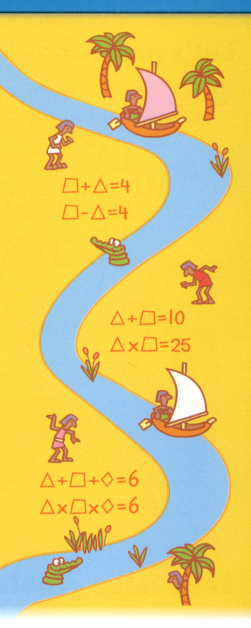

Let's investigate

4. Investigate arranging the digits 2 to 9 in a line so that the difference between touching digits is either 3 or 4.

You need

digit cards for numbers 2 to 9

What if the difference between touching digits was neither 3 nor 4?

Let's practise

1 Write a number story for each number sentence.

13 x 6 = 78   A pen costs 13p.   Six pens cost 78p.

a 78 + 13 = 91   **b** 91 − 56 = 35

c 35 ÷ 7 = 5   **d** 5 x 6 = 30

e 30 ÷ 10 = 3   **f** 3 + 11 = 14

g 14 x 5 = 70   **h** 36 − 23 = 13

Let's play   A game for 2

You need a dice, counters in 2 colours

● Take turns to roll the dice. Use this key to give a sign.

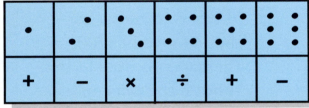

•	∙∙	∙∙∙	∙∙∙∙	∙∙∙∙∙	∙∙∙∙∙∙
+	−	×	÷	+	−

● Find where the sign could go to make a number sentence correct.

● Place a counter on the sentence.

● The winner is the player who covers more number sentences.

23 ★ 64 = 87	30 ★ 3 = 10	43 ★ 28 = 15	27 ★ 3 = 9
10 ★ 8 = 80	40 ★ 20 = 20	12 ★ 2 = 24	16 ★ 15 = 31
36 ★ 6 = 6	51 ★ 28 = 23	36 ★ 6 = 30	26 ★ 32 = 58
7 ★ 5 = 35	26 ★ 2 = 13	72 ★ 25 = 47	63 ★ 3 = 21
4 ★ 90 = 360	40 ★ 6 = 240	19 ★ 21 = 40	83 ★ 56 = 27

Let's practise

1 Copy and complete.

a $\frac{1}{2}$ of 68 = ☐

b   Twice 37 is ☐

c   Half of 84 equals ☐

d   Double 360 is ☐

e   380 divided by 2 equals ☐

f   2 x 3400 = ☐

Let's solve problems

2

a   Jack is twice as old as Ben. Ben is 12. How old is Jack?

b   Dev is half as old as Bill. Bill is 72. How old is Dev?

c   Twice as many people saw United play as saw City. 4700 watched City. How many watched United?

d   Jo wants to buy a car. She has saved £3900. The car costs double this. What is the price of the car?

e   The new Nazda van is double the mass of the old one. The new van weighs 3200 kg. What is the mass of the old van?

f   Half as many people saw Celtic play as saw Rangers. 2700 watched Celtic. How many watched Rangers?

g   There are 390 cars in the car park today. This is half as many as yesterday. How many were there yesterday?

h   On Tuesday 260 birds came to the bird table. This was twice as many as on Monday. How many were there on Monday?

Let's practise

① Work these out mentally.

- ⓐ 86 add 15
- ⓑ 35 take away 12
- ⓒ 90 plus 80
- ⓓ Take 16 from 31.
- ⓔ Find the total of 24 and 76.
- ⓕ Add 63 to 37.
- ⓖ 85 subtract 60
- ⓗ Find the sum of 38 and 17.
- ⓘ Subtract 36 from 75.
- ⓙ Find the difference between 100 and 45.

Let's solve problems

② On holiday, Rifat's friends and family are talking about their ages. Write the age of each person.

- ⓐ In 16 years' time I will be 25.
- ⓑ My daughter is 27 years younger than me. She is 8.
- ⓒ My dad is 4 times as old as me. He is 36.
- ⓓ My daughter is one quarter of my age. One year ago she was 9.
- ⓔ In 6 years' time my aunt will be 54. She is 3 times my age.
- ⓕ In 14 years' time my uncle will be 53. I am one third of his age.

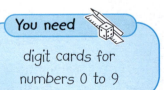

Let's investigate

③ ⓐ Find all the pairs of cards with a sum of 9. How many pairs did you find?

ⓑ Investigate all the pairs of cards with a sum of 8, 7, 6, 5, 4, 3, 2, 1. How many pairs did you find for each sum?

ⓒ Write about any patterns you found.

> **You need**
>
> digit cards for numbers 0 to 9

Let's practise

1 Work these out mentally.

  a Divide 108 by 9.
  b Multiply 32 by 3.
  c Subtract 28 from 62.
  d 48 shared between 6.
  e 19 less than 41.
  f How many groups of 4 in 32?
  g The difference between 41 and 16.
  h The sum of 30, 25 and 45.

Let's solve problems

2 **a** There are 46 videos in the children's section. 27 have been rented out. How many are left to choose from?

  b There are 32 people in the shop. 17 leave but 11 more come in. How many people are in the shop now?

  c If it costs £2·99 to rent 1 video, how much does it cost to rent 3?

  d Today, half the videos in the comedy section are out. There are 29 comedy videos left. How many are there in total?

  e There are 3 shelves each holding 13 videos. Jo rents 4 of them. How many are on the shelves now?

  f There are 4 stacks of videos. 3 stacks have 15 videos each and 1 stack has 10. How many videos are there altogether?

  g These 3 videos are on special offer. Jamil rents 2 of them. How much might he have paid?

£1·75

£1·99

£2·49

Let's practise

1) Use these numbers and words to write as many different correct number sentences as you can.

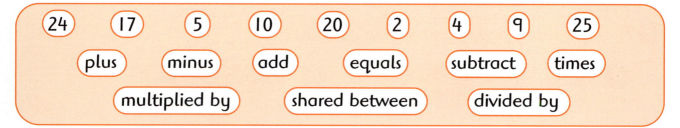

(24) (17) (5) (10) (20) (2) (4) (9) (25)

(plus) (minus) (add) (equals) (subtract) (times)

(multiplied by) (shared between) (divided by)

Let's solve problems

2) Answer the questions. Use the key below to find the letter for each answer. Rearrange the letters to spell a mathematical word.

a) 28 pieces of fruit are in a bowl. 19 are oranges. How many are not oranges?

b) 29 people are on a bus. 13 get off and 22 get on. How many on the bus now?

c) How many legs do 15 cows and 2 birds have?

d) Ann has 30p. Pip has 10p more than twice that amount. How much does Pip have?

e) I think of a number. I add 7 and then multiply by 2. The answer is 26. What is my number?

f) There are 5 times as many sparrows as robins on the bird table. If there are 4 robins, how many birds are on the table?

g) 48 children are on a trip. Half have spring onion crisps. One quarter have plain crisps. How many have other flavours or no crisps?

h) On the trip the girls ate 110 sweets. The boys ate one tenth of that. How many sweets did the boys eat?

Key

6	64	10	8	9	38	70	11	12	24
L	I	B	M	G	A	E	R	T	N

Let's practise

1 Write these amounts in pounds.

 a 642p   **b** 831p   **c** 527p   **d** 607p

2 Find the totals and write them in pounds.

 a

b

c

d

3 Write 3 different ways to pay these prices.

52p   2p, 50p   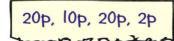 20p, 10p, 20p, 2p   10p, 10p, 10p, 10p, 10p, 2p

a £1·25   **b** £2·40   **c** £1·78   **d** £0·79   **e** 99p

Can you find the smallest number of coins needed?

Let's play   A game for 2

- Each pick 2 cards and find the total.
- Write down your working.

You need

coins and notes cards
from Activity Sheet 33

Card A ... 20p + 50p + 5p + £1 + 1p + 1p = £1·77
Card C ... 5p + 5p + 5p + £2 + £1 + £5 = £8·15
                                    Total   £9·92

- The player with the total closer to £10·00 scores a point.
- The winner is the first to score 5 points.

Let's practise

1 Write how to pay these amounts using the smallest number of coins and notes.

a £3·64

b £1·27

c £2·21

d £1·39

e £4·46

f £9·99

Let's investigate

2 Choose a starting amount between £1 and £5.
Follow this trail.

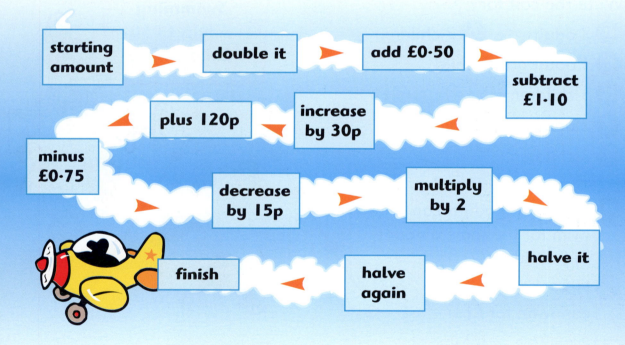

starting amount ► double it ► add £0·50 ►

subtract £1·10

◄ plus 120p ◄ increase by 30p ◄

minus £0·75

► decrease by 15p ► multiply by 2 ►

halve it

◄ finish ◄ halve again ◄

- Write down your trail.

£1·60 ⟶ £3·20 ⟶ £3·70 ⟶ £2·60⟶

- What do you notice about your starting and finishing amounts?

Repeat several times, choosing different starting amounts.

Let's practise

1 Write the fewest notes and coins needed to pay exactly for each activity.

a £8·53

b £6·03

c £4·92

d £11·38

Let's solve problems

2 Write the cost for

   a 2 adults   **b** 2 children

   c 1 adult and 1 child

   d 3 children

   e 2 adults and 3 children

   f 8 children.

Swimming
Adults £1·50
Children 75p

3 **a** How many adults can swim for the same amount as 8 children?

   b How many children can swim for £12?

Let's investigate

4 In my purse I have 1 note and 3 identical coins. Investigate how much money could be in my purse.

    £5, 1p, 1p, 1p ➞ £5·03

? What if I have 3 notes and 1 coin in my purse?

Let's practise

1. a) Write each length in 3 ways.

   A is 1 cm 2 mm or 1·2 cm or 12 mm

   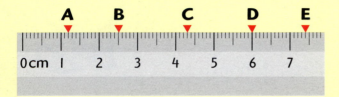

   b) Draw a line that is:
      - 8 cm longer than length A
      - 8 cm longer than length C
      - 65 mm longer than length B
      - 65 mm longer than length D.

2. Draw triangles with the lengths shown below for 2 of the sides.
   Measure the third side.
   Write the length of each side in 2 ways.

   a) 3 cm and 4 cm
   b) 45 mm and 50 mm
   c) 37 mm and 6 cm
   d) 7·5 cm and 62 mm

3. Draw these polygons. Make each side at least 2·5 cm.

   a) quadrilateral
   b) pentagon
   c) hexagon

   Measure and write the length of each side in millimetres.

Let's investigate

4. Investigate using the sticks in the box to measure whole-number centimetre lengths from 2 cm to 25 cm.
   Record your findings.

Let's practise

1 Choose the best measurement
from the box below for

a the height of a bus wheel

b the length of a goods train

c the distance between 2 railway stations

d the height of overhead signs above a motorway.

| 10km | 1km | 100m | 10m | 1m | 10cm |

Let's solve problems

2 The Robertsons drove over these passes in the Canadian Rockies.

a Copy and complete the table.

Pass	Height above sea level (metres)	Rounded to the nearest 10m	Rounded to the nearest 100m
Yellowhead	1066m	1070m	1100m
Kicking Horse	1643m		
Crow's Nest	1382m		
Monashee	1189m		
Vermilion	1637m		
Roger's	1327m		

b How many metres higher
is Kicking Horse Pass than

- Crow's Nest Pass

- Monashee Pass?

c Which 2 passes have a difference in height of 55 metres?

d A mile is approximately 1600 metres.
Which of the passes are more than 1 mile above sea level?

Let's practise

1.

   50 g   **100 g**   **200 g**   **500 g**

   Use these standard masses to measure the mass of each box.
   Choose the smallest number of masses for each.

   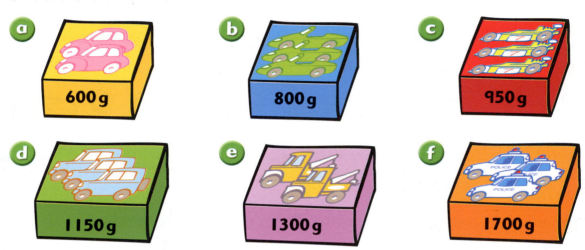

   a. 600 g
   b. 800 g
   c. 950 g
   d. 1150 g
   e. 1300 g
   f. 1700 g

2. Write the mass of each toy rounded to the nearest 100 g.

   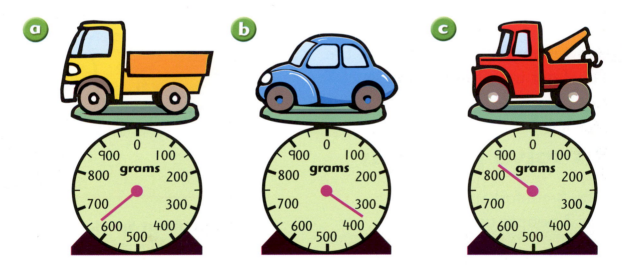

   a
   b
   c

Let's investigate

3. Imagine that you have only one of each of these
   masses: 50 g, 100 g, 500 g. Investigate using them
   to balance objects with a mass of 50 g, 100 g,
   150 g, 200 g, ... up to 500 g. Which are impossible?

   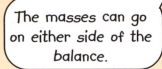

   The masses can go
   on either side of the
   balance.

Let's practise

Food mass per portion

Frosty Flakes	50 g	chef's salad	175 g
yoghurt	125 g	sausage and egg	150 g
banana	150 g	beefburger	75 g
soup	70 g	baked potato	250 g
baked beans	60 g	French fries	100 g

1 Find the total mass of food on each tray, in grams.

a 　**b** 　**c** 　**d**

2 One egg has a mass of about 50 g. There are 10 eggs in a box.
What is the mass of:

a 2 eggs　　　**b** 4 eggs　　　**c** 10 eggs

d 2 boxes of eggs　　**e** 5 boxes　　**f** 10 boxes?

3 How many 100 g portions will the
chef get from this bag of French fries?

FROZEN
French Fries
5.5kg

Let's solve problems

4 The Breakfast Special
for **2** people uses:

5 × 50 g eggs　　　100 g toast
60 g tomatoes　　　40 g mushrooms.

a Write the list above with
the quantities for 4 people.

b Find the total mass of this order.

Breakfast Special
fried eggs
fried tomatoes
button mushrooms
buttered toast

Let's practise

6 l 250 ml

① These dipsticks show the fuel left in each boat engine.

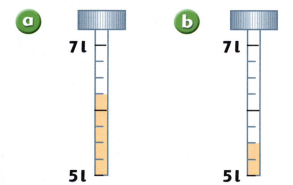

a 7 l 5 l

b 7 l 5 l

c 8 l 6 l

d 10 l 9 l

Write each reading in 3 different ways.

6 l 250 ml   6250 ml $6\frac{1}{4}$ l

② The readings show how much fuel is in each go-kart engine.
Copy and complete the table.

Go-kart	Fuel in ml	Fuel in l
Amber	400 ml	$\frac{4}{10}$ l
Bravo		
Champ		
Dragon		
Excel		
Firefly		

Dragon — 1000 ml
Firefly — 800 ml
Bravo — 600 ml
Amber — 400 ml
Champ — 200 ml
Excel —

Let's investigate

③ Investigate filling whole number litre
containers from 1 l to 30 l using these jugs.
The jugs cannot be partly full.
Record your findings.

1 l   2 l
4 l   8 l

Let's practise

1 Find the number of times you can fill each measure from the large container next to it.

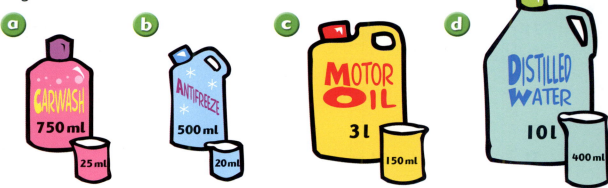

a CARWASH 750 ml — 25 ml
b ANTIFREEZE 500 ml — 20 ml
c MOTOR OIL 3 l — 150 ml
d DISTILLED WATER 10 l — 400 ml

2 A pint is about half a litre.

   a How many pints of water are there in the 10 litre container?

   b How many pints of oil can you get from the 3 litre can?

Let's solve problems

3 Bimla checks the oil in her car.
She buys a 3 l can and uses up 600 ml.

   a How many times does she fill the yellow 150 ml oil measure?

   b How much oil is left in the can?

4 The mechanic makes a pot of tea.

250ml
1·5 l
150 ml

   a How many mugs of tea can he pour?

   b How much tea is left in the pot after he fills 3 mugs and 2 cups?

5 Bimla buys 3 cans of cola and 6 cartons of orange. How much drink does she buy in litres and millilitres?

250 ml   330 ml

Let's practise

1 Work out the perimeter of each shape.

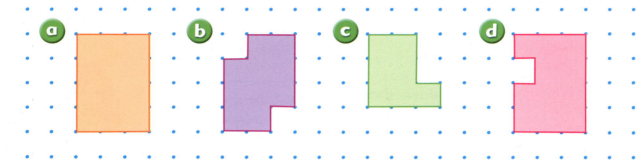

2 For each perimeter below, draw 2 different rectangles.

a perimeter 10 cm

b perimeter 14 cm

c perimeter 18 cm

d perimeter 22 cm

e perimeter 24 cm

You need

pinboard, rubber band, ruler, square dotty paper

Use your pinboard to find the rectangles.

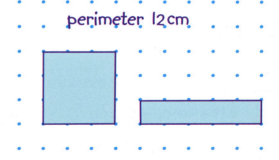

perimeter 12 cm

Let's investigate

3 Use square dotty paper to investigate drawing as many of each of these shapes as you can. Each shape must have a 16 cm perimeter.

a rectangle

b irregular hexagon

c irregular octagon

How many of each shape did you draw?

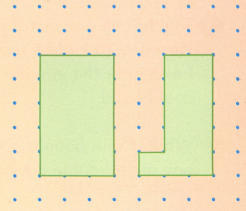

Let's practise

1 • Choose 3 different covering units.

• Work out the area of this page using each one.

You need covering units of the same size, such as squares, dominoes, playing cards

2 **a** Find the area of each shape.

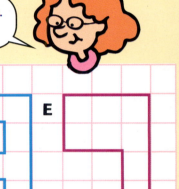

Count the small squares. A is 8 square units.

A B C D E

F

G

b Which shape above has:

• the smallest area
• the greatest area
• twice the area of shape B
• 5 squares less than the largest area?

c Which shapes above have the same areas?

Let's investigate

3 Saul has 48 one metre square paving stones. He wants to build a rectangular patio. Investigate the possible sizes of patio he could build.

? What if Saul bought another 12 one metre square paving stones?

Let's practise

1 Write each time in 2 ways.

a   b   c   d

17 minutes past 9 or 9:17

2 Look at the time on the station clock.
Write the time in digital form

a 3 minutes later

b in 3 hours' time

c 3 hours earlier

d in 30 minutes' time

e half an hour ago.

Let's solve problems

3 Read the clues to choose the correct time.
For each one, sketch the analogue clock face and draw the time you chose.

a in the afternoon
before 6 pm
after quarter to 5

| 6:10 pm | 5:43 am |
| 4:45 pm | 5:48 pm |

b before midday
at least 2 hours after 9 am
odd number of minutes

| 10:53 am | 11:35 am |
| 12:35 pm | 11:44 am |

c Write 3 clues so that the time is 9:27 pm.

Let's practise

| 4:37 | 37 minutes past 4 | 23 minutes to 5 |

1 Write these times in 2 ways.

a 6:40   **b** 5:43   **c** 10:51   **d** 2:28   **e** 12:56

Let's solve problems

2 **a** Copy and complete the table to show the digital finish time for each rally car.

46 21 minutes to 4
39 28 minutes past 3
22 35 minutes past 3
35 14 minutes to 4
20 28 minutes to 4
65 7 minutes to 4

Spotlight Car Rally
Forest stage results

Car	Finish time
46	3:39
39	

b How many minutes after the winner did the last car finish?

3 Here are the results for the mountain stage of the race. Work out the finish time for each car.

| car 46   12:10 am |

Car	Start time	Time for mountain stage
46	10:00 pm	2 hours 10 minutes
39	10:05 pm	1 hour 45 minutes
22	10:10 pm	1 hour 57 minutes
35	10:15 pm	2 hours 12 minutes
20	10:20 pm	2 hours 2 minutes
65	10:25 pm	1 hour 59 minutes

Let's solve problems

1 The ferry sails between the mainland and the island. The crossing takes 15 minutes.
It takes 10 minutes to unload and load the vehicles.

Look for patterns to help you.

Copy and complete this timetable.

Leave mainland ➤ Arrive island		Leave island ➤ Arrive mainland	
9:00	9:15	9:25	9:40
9:50		10:15	
10:40		11:05	
	11:45		12:10
		12:45	

2 Where is the ferry at:

a 10 o'clock   **b** 11 o'clock

c 12 o'clock   **d** 1 o'clock?

3 The ferry does not sail on Sundays.

a Write the dates in July and August when it does not sail.

July						
S	M	T	W	Th	F	Sa
				1	2	3
4	5	6	7	8	9	10
11	12	13	14	15	16	17
18	19	20	21	22	23	24
25	26	27	28	29	30	31

August						
S	M	T	W	Th	F	Sa
1	2	3	4	5	6	7
8	9	10	11	12	13	14
15	16	17	18	19	20	21
22	23	24	25	26	27	28
29	30	31				

b On which of these dates will there be no ferry to the island?

You need
a calendar for May this year

6 May   12 May   14 May   18 May   22 May   24 May   30 May

Let's practise

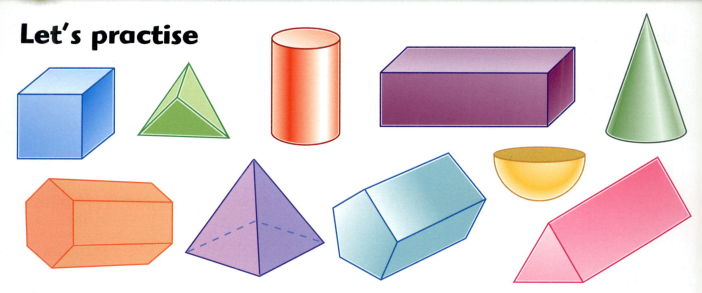

1 Name the shape that:

   a has 4 vertices and only triangular faces

   b has 6 edges on an end face and 12 vertices

   c has 1 square face and 8 edges

   d is a prism and has 5 faces.

2 Write 1 more fact about each shape in question 1.

Let's solve problems

You need

interlocking cubes

3 • Estimate the smallest number of cubes you need to build each shape.
  • Build each shape.
  • Record the number of cubes you used.

  a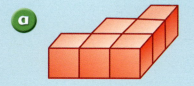

  b

  c

  d

  e

  f

Let's practise

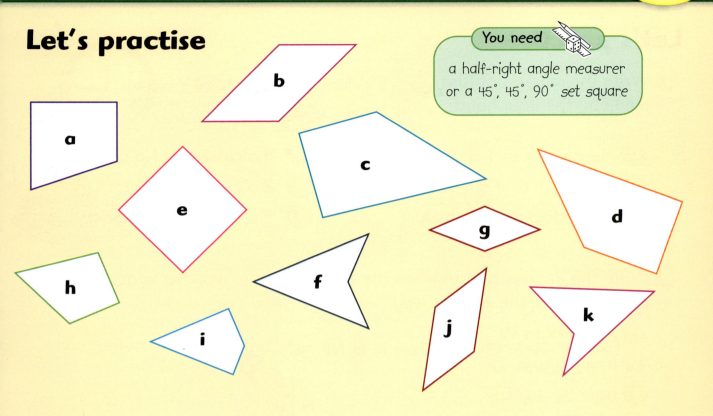

1. Write the letters of the shapes that have:

   a) 1 angle of 90°   b) 2 angles of 90°

   c) 4 angles of 90°   d) no angles of 90°.

2. Write the letters of the shapes that have:

   a) 1 angle of 45°   b) 2 angles of 45°.

Let's investigate

3. Investigate this statement:

It is possible to make 11 different shapes
by placing 4 identical right-angled
triangles equal side against equal side.

Here are 3 of the shapes.
Find more shapes.
Draw each shape you find on dotty paper.

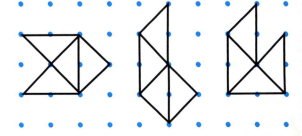

Let's practise

1 Write the amount of turn made by the hour hand.

3 o'clock to 5 o'clock: 60°

60°

  a 12 o'clock to 1 o'clock

  b 9 o'clock to 11 o'clock

  c 5 o'clock to 8 o'clock

  d 2 o'clock to 6 o'clock

  e 11 o'clock to 3 o'clock

  f 9 o'clock to 2 o'clock

2 Write the degrees of turn when the wind blows the weather vane. It always turns the shortest way.

  a from SW to W

  b from SE to E

  c from NE to SE

  d from NW to SW

  e from SE to NW

  f from N to SE

  g from NE to W

from N to NE: 45°

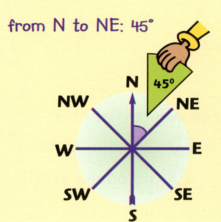

Let's play   A game for 2

Take turns to:

- Point the pencil to a direction on the compass.

- Say which way the pencil is pointing.

- Roll the dice. C means turn clockwise.
  A means turn anticlockwise.

- Ask your partner to say the direction the pencil will point to after making the turn shown by the dice.

- Turn the pencil to check.
  A correct answer scores 1 point.

- The winner is the first with 8 points.

You need

a pencil, a compass made from a paper circle, a dice marked 45°A, 45°C, 90°A, 90°C, 135°A, 135°C

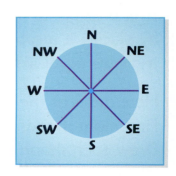

Let's investigate

 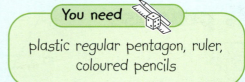
1 Draw around the perimeter of a regular pentagon. Use your ruler to draw lines from 1 vertex to the 2 vertices opposite.

Find an isosceles triangle. Colour it in. Find a different isosceles triangle. Colour it in a different colour.

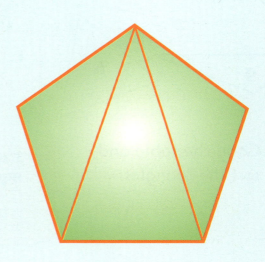

2 Draw another pentagon. Use a ruler to draw 3 lines, as shown.

Find 2 isosceles triangles that are different from those in question 1. Colour 1 triangle. Colour the second triangle a different colour.

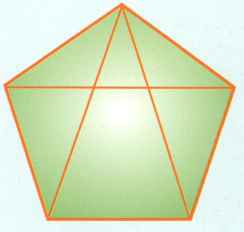

3 Draw a third pentagon. Carefully draw lines from each vertex to the 2 vertices opposite.

a How many isosceles triangles are there?

b How many different isosceles triangles are there?

Let's practise

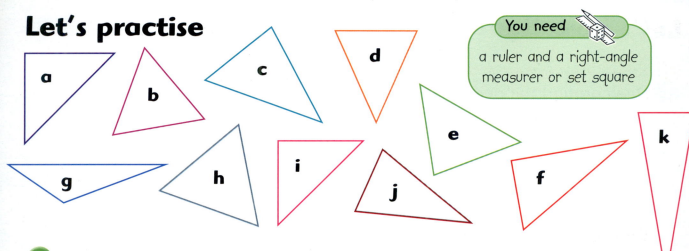

> **You need**
>
> a ruler and a right-angle measurer or set square

1 Copy the table and sort the triangles.

3 sides equal	Only 2 sides equal	No sides equal
b	d	

2 Copy the Venn diagram and sort the triangles.

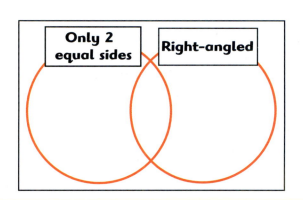

Only 2 equal sides   Right-angled

Let's investigate

> **You need**
>
> a pinboard, rubber bands and square dotty paper

3 Investigate making different triangles on a 3 x 3 pinboard.

   a Draw the triangles you make on dotty paper.
Name any that are right-angled, isosceles or equilateral triangles.
Write whether each one has a line of symmetry.

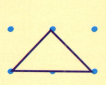

   b Which type of triangle cannot be made on your pinboard?

a right-angled isosceles triangle
1 line of symmetry

Let's practise

You need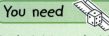
8 identical right-angled isosceles triangles, square dotty paper, ruler

1 Take 2 of the triangles and join them to make:

a a square

b a right-angled triangle.

Draw the 2 shapes on dotty paper.

2 Take 4 of the triangles and join them to make:

a a rectangle

b a square

c a right-angled triangle.

Draw the 3 shapes on dotty paper.

3 Take 6 of the triangles and join them to make:

a a pentagon

b a hexagon.

Draw the 2 shapes on dotty paper.

Join matching straight sides

Let's investigate

4 Investigate different shapes you can make using all 8 triangles.

Draw each shape you make on dotty paper.

? What if you had 8 identical equilateral triangles?

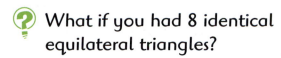

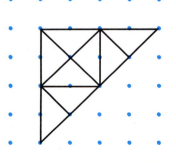

Let's solve problems

1 The table shows the number of children in Weston School in one week.

Year	M	T	W	Th	F
3	28	27	29	24	18
4	30	32	32	26	21
5	30	29	30	22	20
6	27	30	31	25	22

a There was a full attendance in all 4 classes on Wednesday. How many children were not at school on Monday?

b How many children were at school on Tuesday?

c On which day was attendance at school the lowest?

d How many children were absent that day? Why do you think so many children were not at school?

Let's investigate

2 Ask your teacher for information about the number of children present in your class for each day over the last 3 weeks.

- Make a table of the data.

- Write 3 questions about the data.

- Swap questions with a partner and write the answers.

Let's practise

1 **a** Write the numbers shown by these tallies.

Common words	Tally
a	LHT LHT III
and	LHT LHT LHT LHT
he	LHT LHT I
it	LHT I
the	LHT LHT II
to	LHT III

b Which word occurred

- most often
- least often?

Let's investigate

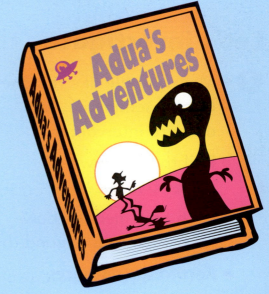

You need

a reading book

2 • Choose a page of the reading book.

• Predict which word from the list below will
occur most often and which least often on that page.

a	and	he
it	the	to

- Draw a tally chart for the words and
  complete it.

- Did you predict correctly?

- In what ways is your chart the same as
  (or different from) the one in question 1?

? What if you chose a different book?

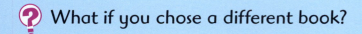

Let's solve problems

1 Shabana rolled a car down a slope 50 times.

Each time she recorded how far the car rolled beyond the end of the slope.

Distance rolled	Number of times
80 cm or less	4
81–100 cm	12
101–120 cm	10
121–140 cm	6
141–160 cm	15
161–180 cm	3

a Which distance did the car roll most often?

b Which distance did the car roll least often?

c How many times did the car roll more than 100 cm?

d Why do you think the car rolled 121–140 cm only 6 times?

Let's investigate

You need

a toy car, a slope, a tape measure

2 ● Make a table like this one. Choose sensible distance intervals.

Distance rolled	Number of times	
	First 50 times	Second 50 times

● Roll the car down the slope 50 times.

● Each time measure how far the car rolls beyond the end of the slope.

● Record the distances.

● Repeat this for another 50 times.

● Write about any differences between your 2 sets of results.

Let's practise

1 Copy and complete.

a $2 + 2 = \square$ **b** $2 + 2 + 2 + 2 + 1 = \square$ **c** $2 + 2 + 2 + 2 = \square$

2 Write each of the numbers in the box as the sum of 2s and, if necessary, a 1.

7	15	6	
31	19	10	23

$7 = 2 + 2 + 2 + 1$

Let's solve problems

3 This pictogram shows the number of aeroplanes that flew over Blue Sky School one week.

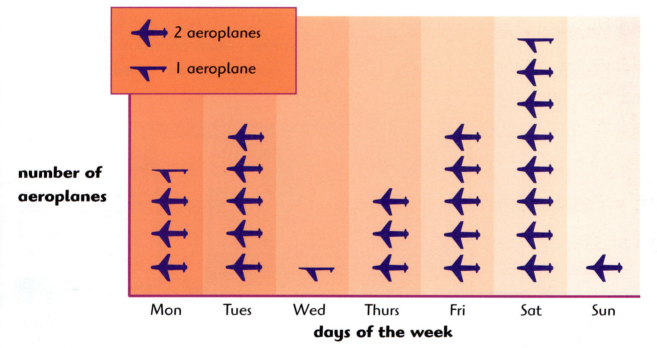

a Write the number of aeroplanes that flew over each day.

b Which were the least busy days?

c Why do you think Saturday was the busiest day?

d Which 2 days were the same?

e Write 3 statements about what the pictogram shows.

Let's solve problems

1 The graph shows the colours of cars that drove past Beam School on Wednesday morning.

a How many red cars passed the school?

b Which colour was twice as common as silver?

c Which colour was half as common as blue?

d How many cars passed the school altogether?

e Use each of the 5 words once only to write 5 sentences about the graph.

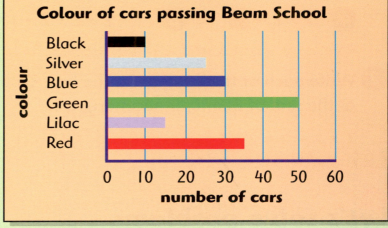

Colour of cars passing Beam School

colour

Black
Silver
Blue
Green
Lilac
Red

0 10 20 30 40 50 60
number of cars

difference   least common

less   most common   more

Let's investigate

2 Make a traffic survey of the different kinds of vehicle that pass your school in 15 minutes.

? What if you did the survey on another day?

Let's practise

1. • Copy the grid of numbers.

   • Tick the multiples of 4.

   • Draw a ring around the multiples of 3.

   • What is special about the numbers with a tick **and** a ring?

21	9	12	16	18
15	10	24	11	14
17	36	13	20	90

Let's investigate

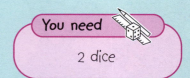

You need

2 dice

2. Work with a partner.

   • Roll both dice and make two 2-digit numbers

   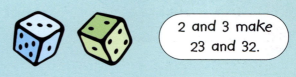

   2 and 3 make 23 and 32.

   • Follow the arrows on the sorting diagram.

   • Decide which boxes your numbers belong in: A, B, C or D.

   • Keep a record.

   • Continue until you have sorted 16 different numbers.

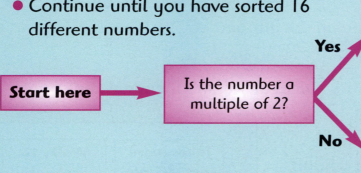

3. Write whether these statements are true or false.

   a. There are no A numbers.

   b. All the B numbers are odd.

   c. All the C numbers are odd.

   d. Any D numbers are multiples of 2, but not multiples of 5.

❓ What if the numbers in the sorting diagram were 3 and 6?

Let's solve problems

Work with a partner.
Stefan found out how his friends travel to school each day. He made this Carroll diagram.

	Takes 20 min or less to get to school	Does not take 20 min or less to get to school
Walks to school	Jamie Sam Rebecca Jeanette Paula	Fiona Madhur Hilary Julian Christa Peter
Does not walk to school	Toby Sarah Tom	Vicki Deepak Harry John

1 **a** How many children take more than 20 minutes to get to school?

   b How many children do not walk to school?

   c How many children walk for more than 20 minutes to get to school?

   d How many children did Stefan ask altogether?

2 Draw a Venn diagram. Write the names of Stefan's friends in the correct places on your Venn diagram.

   a How many children take more than 20 minutes to get to school?

   b How many children do not walk to school?

   c How many children walk for more than 20 minutes to get to school?

   d How many children did Stefan ask altogether?

Takes more than 20 min	Walks to school

Compare your answers for questions 1 and 2.
What do you notice?
Explain why.